PETERSFIELD
A HUNDRED YEARS AGO

PETERSFIELD FROM TOWER OF ST. PETER'S CHURCH.

David Jeffery

© 2012 David Jeffery
Petersfield A Hundred Years ago

ISBN 978-0-9564290-1-8

Published by David Jeffery Publications
27 Woodbury Avenue
Petersfield
GU32 2ED

A CIP catalogue record of this book
can be obtained from the British Library.

Book designed by Michael Walsh at
THE BETTER BOOK COMPANY
5 Lime Close
Chichester
PO19 6SW

and printed by
ASHFORD COLOUR PRESS
166 Fareham Road
Gosport
Hants PO13 0FW

Contents

Life in Petersfield; Agricultural matters; The Petersfield
Scrap Book; Education; The Press; Cultural and leisure
activities; Local and national politics; New buildings in the
town; Queen Victoria's Diamond Jubilee; Sanitation problems;
The town Fire Brigade; The Union Workhouse; The railway
level crossing; The future of the market; The isolation hospital;
The Boer Wars; Early closing; Street lighting;
Society marriages; Deaths

Introduction; The Coronation of Edward VII; The Boer War; The
Petersfield Musical Festival; The Churches; Education; The Scouting
movement; Fairs and shows; Crime and the Police;
The market question; The Heath; Commercial life; Cultural,
leisure and sporting pursuits; A local Olympian; Public utilities and
services; Road and rail improvements; Social and Technological progress;
Local and National politics; Deaths

Introduction; The Coronation of George V; Sale of the Hylton Estate;
The restoration of the statue of William III; The demolition of Castle
House; The Suffragette movement; Leisure pursuits; Accidents; Changes and
improvements in public amenities in 1912; Sir Heath Harrison; Deaths; War!

Rushes
Farm

60
1·187

59
1·271

226

B.M.222·4

218

219

G.Ps

218

122
·647

FENNS ROAD

Stone
227

S.B.

R.C.Chu
B.M.2

Volunteer
Arms
(P.H.)

F.B.

B.M.229·6

Cr.

Station

Hotel

Web
Church

S

LAVANT STREET

Laundry

W

Cattle
Pens

Goods
Shed

CHARLES STREET

129
2·345

126   218

127
3·198

126
·269

117
·857

118
2·214

B.M.207·9

Allotment Gardens
155
15·843

S.P

156
1·039

M.P

B.M.216·1

167
·616

Salvation
Army
Barracks

210

B.M.214·4

Borough Farm
Buildings
148
8·036

147

F.B.

149
·994

W

158
1·849

157
·949

166
·662

Brewery

220

168
·168

Highfield House

165
2·935

169
·873

170
·718

Cottage Hospital

171
·461

B.M.207·7

Cast

W

Borough Hill House
B.M.228·9   216

THE BOROUGH

164
·863

THE SPAIN
203

B.M.204·1

Borough Hill
160
165

159
2·143

Sand Pit

Old
Sand Pit

ROAD

163
2·644

Stone

172
·460

153
3·372

161
·427

Stone

173
4·501

S.P

150
1·888

151
1·364

152
3·744

162
3·116

PETERSFIELD

Ford

St.

St.

St.

214
16·336

St.

210
11·888

The Gr

Front cover painting –
"Market Day, Petersfield" by William Gunning King

reproduced by courtesy of Portsmouth City Museum

William Gunning King (1859-1940) trained as an artist at South Kensington (now the Royal College of Art) and exhibited regularly at the Royal Academy before moving with his wife to Rock Cottage in Harting in 1885. He soon became involved in the world of commercial art and the Liverpool milling firm of Joseph Bibby employed him to advertise their cattle cake and to do illustrations for their company calendars. His homely farming scenes and village greens satisfied the firm's requirements for thirty years, most of his models being local Harting village people. He also painted cards for Raphael Tuck and cartoons for *Punch*. St. Peter's Church in Petersfield houses his painting "Follow me", painted in memory of his wife, for which the figure of Christ was modelled by Fred Lee, the Petersfield Square hairdresser. Gunning King is buried in Harting.

Note on the author

Since retiring as a Modern Languages lecturer, David Jeffery has published two histories of Petersfield: *Petersfield at War* (2004) and *Postwar Petersfield* (2006); one brief biography: *Harry Roberts – a Petersfield philanthropist* (2009); the history of *Petersfield and Sheet Scouts and Guides* (2007); and co-authored a concise history of the town: *The Story of Petersfield* (2009). He has also co-produced six DVDs for Angerton Video Productions, including a tribute to the poet *Edward Thomas* for the Edward Thomas Fellowship and an account of the *Arts and Crafts Movement in Steep and Petersfield*, sponsored by Bedales School.

Introduction

A description of rural England in the Victorian era would inevitably contain references to the hierarchy of landlord, tenant and labourer which had pertained since the late eighteenth century and which had established a set of social values to last for the whole century.

On the positive side, the hierarchy had provided the structure to improve cultivation and to increase expenditure on the great estates; at the same time, however, it embodied a system which had led to two major class struggles: the labourers' struggle against the farmer for higher wages and the farmers' struggle against the landlord for lower rents. The former of these had resulted in the formation of the trade union movement in the 1870s, and the concomitant improvement – albeit slow – of working conditions, yet the latter gave rise to very few serious confrontations, a phenomenon mainly attributable to the bond of personal affection that had drawn together the local squires and their farmers. The situation in Petersfield was not dissimilar to this pattern of living: the Lords of the Manor generally held sway over their communities and there was an implicit deference paid to them by the community.

The Victorian era had produced smart houses of red brick to replace the solid stone or flimsy wood and plaster of the old cottages; railway trains expelled the stage coaches; old packhorse tracks were now well-paved roads; great new towns and new industries grew up; trains, motor cars and bicycles transformed the manners and customs of the people even in the remotest corners of Hampshire, as elsewhere. This slow but noticeable metamorphosis of the county made itself particularly felt in Petersfield, where all the elements which went to create these changes were present: first, the railway, then the new housing developments; the humble bicycle and the status-conscious motor car; paved roads and street lighting; town design and gradual urbanisation. But Petersfield has always clung to its past glories – its medieval town layout, its ancient buildings, the rural aspects of its Heath, the agricultural focus of its market, its compact form within a large swathe of naturally beautiful scenery.

By the end of the Victorian era, fewer than four per cent of the population of Hampshire were engaged in agriculture or associated trades. By the time of the First World War, still only about a tenth of agricultural land was farmed by owner-occupiers. Brewing was one of the chief industries of Petersfield; the largest breweries were Luker's and Amey's and the Square Brewery was just that, as well as a public house. Two nearby villages specialised in hop-growing: Col. Bonham-Carter was well-established at Buriton, as was Charles Seward at Weston.

The average rural resident would ride or even walk many miles to buy or sell their agricultural produce: milk and butter, fruit and vegetables, cattle and other livestock at the market. Likewise, children would walk long distances to school and sometimes go home for lunch and back again for their afternoon classes.

Some respite from this everyday toil was had from the inventions of the decade such as the vacuum cleaner and the wireless, while horizons were expanding with the coming of the telephone and the motor car. Entertainments, too, were changing: shopping became a pastime instead of a necessity: national chains of stores and department stores emerged, such as Boots, Freeman, Hardy and Willis, Lipton's – and the Marks and Spencer partnership began in 1894. It was the birth of the "generic High Street". Horse power turned into electric power, but the existence of the two concurrent means of locomotion often led to chaos on the streets and this was further exacerbated with the passing of the Locomotives on the Highway Act of 1896, which removed the requirement for a man to walk in front of cars, thus raising the speed limit from four to fourteen miles per hour.

While most folk were hard-working, even earnest in their endeavours, there was clearly a sense of social hierarchy and dignity about the nation which translated itself into patriotism, consciousness of Britain's vast Empire, and the love of a seemingly immortal Queen. In a strictly stratified society, however, the labouring classes were not living out an idyll. With farms becoming vacant, cottages falling into dereliction and hard-working tenants in short supply, country life at the beginning of the twentieth century was about eking out a living from an agricultural sector which had been in sporadic crisis since the 1870s. It was hardly surprising that many young families chose to emigrate.

Within the context of gender roles, there was the unacceptable concept of women working (although working-class women did find jobs in domestic service and manufacturing and their middle-class equivalents went into teaching or nursing). The advent of typewriters in the 1890s created so-called "lady typewriters" and there was an increasing call for (women) telephone operators.

The rich began to build themselves detached villas – perhaps to ape the domestic independence of the upper classes – thus contributing to what became known as "Villa Toryism", while the labouring classes, especially in rural areas, followed the rhythm of the countryside as they had done for centuries. This was more like an eking out of a humdrum existence than real living, as thousands suffered from the agricultural doldrums of the age. When wheat prices fell in 1894, thousands were forced off the land and headed for the cities or emigrated to the English-speaking countries of the Empire. A downturn in international trade and growing foreign competition brought industrial disputes and gave rise to the Trade Union Movement before the century was out, which, in its turn, was to bring about the first structuring of the welfare state.

Nikolaus Pevsner called Hampshire's Victorian and Edwardian eras "a bumper period" when, against the county's predominantly agricultural background, the arrival of the railway in mid-century placed the towns and villages within easy reach of London, thus leading to mild urban expansion and allowing businessmen and entrepreneurs to take over and improve existing country estates. Middle-class city dwellers began to move out and populate these new residences and Petersfield was typical of such an area within this commercial and demographic shift.

Then, as now and, undoubtedly as it ever will be, the underlying conflict between material growth and moral progress was being waged and debated in forums of all political persuasions. Between the excesses and extremes of the rich and the poor lay the middle classes, the commercial and business classes, which still provide politicians with their raison d'être today. Plus ça change...

Petersfield a hundred years ago is an attempt to bring a dose of reality to the sometimes distorted (or at least rose-tinted) view of the age currently presented in the media, thanks to which we run the risk of wallowing in unrealistic nostalgia – escapism for escapism's sake. By contrast, this book's historical reliance on everyday press accounts, personal reminiscences and contemporary pictures of people and events is intended to bring that era more accurately to life. The quarter century thus depicted aims to reflect the social, political, intellectual, cultural and technological forces at work in one small town in Hampshire, one that was decisively buffeted by these changes and which responded for good or ill towards them.

The oldest known photograph of Petersfield High Street (c.1880)

CHAPTER ONE

The late Victorian era

Life in Petersfield

harles Harper, in his 1895 book on *The Portsmouth Road*, seems to emphasise the somnolence of Petersfield with some relish:

> "[Petersfield's] market is but fortnightly, and for thirteen days out of every fourteen, the town dozes tranquilly. The imagination pictures the inhabitants of this old to municipal and parliamentary borough rubbing their eyes and and yawning every alternate Wednesday, when the corn and cattle market is held; and when the last drover has gone, at the close of day, sinking again into slumber with a sigh of relief".

However, even some of the town's own inhabitants must have shared this disparaging opinion, for, in a retrospective speech given at the Petersfield Working Men's Club and Institute in 1896, Dr Leachman, the well-known and very active Petersfield doctor and local councillor, made the comment that, a quarter of a century before, the town had not been a very desirable place to live in, that it was, in short, "deadly dull". There had been no athletic or football clubs (there was a cricket club, but the Petersfield Football Club was not founded until 1889); the Corn Exchange (which was to become, after 1866, the prime venue for many types of recreational and cultural events) was not built; and evening entertainments were conspicuous by their absence.

The Square in Victorian times, drawn by Charles Harper

The old cricket pavilion, built 1881, destroyed by fire in 1973

Despite this apparent lack of facilities for the general population, it must be mentioned that working men did have their own centre for their recreational and sporting needs: the above-mentioned Working Men's Club and Institute – an honest and typically Victorian appellation – had begun life in mid-century for those men who had little money to spend on entertainment. Run (also characteristically for the era) by the local vicar and dignitaries, it provided a library (for self-improvement), bagatelle and billiards, and held occasional lectures.

When, in 1886, it obtained its first dedicated building [now the Scout Hut] for its activities, thanks to the philanthropic generosity of Lord Hylton, it began to build up its membership to 50 members.

The (former) Working Men's Institute in Heath Road

In 1894, the Petersfield Literary and Debating Society, which had been founded ten years earlier, heard Mr Joseph Richardson, a relative newcomer to the town, give a talk entitled "Some pessimistic views of Petersfield", a provocative title, deliberately chosen so that he could refute some previously expressed opinions on the town as "sleepy", "miserable" and "unprogressive". Worse, some had talked of the town as one pervaded by "cliques, caste and bigotry". However, the speaker dismissed these comments as the rantings of pessimists and "croakers" – he felt that the District Local Board [the predecessor to the Urban District Council] had the right men in the Council chamber and that the town had before it a future brightening in every sense, "whether in its commercial prosperity, its attractions as a place of residence or its social harmony". Two years previously, Mr Richardson said, there had been a certain temporary stagnation in the affairs of Petersfield, but this was no doubt the result of the influenza epidemic which had been prevalent for some months that year.

In the ensuing debate – a fine feature of this particular society in the late Victorian era – speakers praised the efforts and improvements brought about by "a determined few". For example, it was thanks to Lord Hylton's munificence that the Working Men's Club had been built in Heath Road in 1886, and whose example was followed by the creation of an equivalent Institute for women in 1900.

The town did on occasion sink into lethargy, but this was enlivened by a few bright moments, as a report at Easter 1892 reveals: "Eastertide at P. has as usual been a very quiet period, and combined at times with the depressing weather, it can be regarded as exceptionally dull. On Monday, there were scarcely any public diversions, although the large number of cyclists which passed through the town on that day, as on the 3 days previous, and the arrival of a number of Salvationists with their band, imparted a little movement to the otherwise comparatively deserted streets."

The more optimistic and positive critics among the town's residents hoped for improvements in the life of Petersfield, especially in the development of the "exquisite pleasure ground" of the Heath; commercial advertising of the town at railway stations and other much-frequented centres of population to make Petersfield known to "the toilers of the Metropolis"; intellectual improvement by the establishment of "a good Athenaeum"; a moral benefit in the creation of a vigorous and progressive temperance society; and religious improvement by the establishment of Sunday afternoon services, "services with plenty of music and brief addresses"; and, finally, a call for the creation of a town Museum.

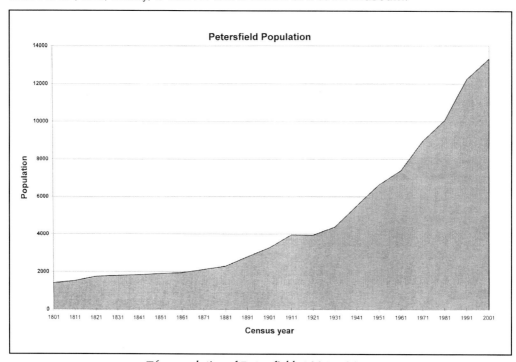

The population of Petersfield, 1801 – 2001

Petersfield's population in the 1890s was a little below 3,000. There had been a noticeable increase the previous decade with the construction of houses the length of Lavant Street and Charles Street, prosperous new four-bedroom villas and terraces in Station Road and new villas and shops in Chapel Street, which indicates that the town was increasing both in population and prosperity. Between 1881 and 1891, the town's population rose by 300, although the rural population had decreased considerably during the same period. There had also been some

College Street stick factory (second building on the left)

increase due to new staff working in Mr Houghton Brown's walking stick factory in College Street, a large number of whom were strangers to the town, and to "the immigration of van people", who had settled in vans and tents near the Heath.

The number of houses in the Urban District Council area in 1896 was 605. The infant death rate was defined as "too high" in a report in the mid-1890s, and this was attributed to improper feeding, diarrhoea, wasting and convulsions. In addition, many children at this time died of typhoid, scarlet fever, tuberculosis and diphtheria.

In the 1880's, the number of children attending the Board School (which had replaced the National School some years before), was 250, but, in the following ten years, a new boys' school and an enlarged infants' school had brought the attendances up to over 500. At the same time, Churcher's College saw its pupil numbers increase from 34 boys when it opened on Ramshill in 1881, to 77 at the end of the century.

Certain long-standing members of the community, Captain the Hon. Sidney Hylton Jolliffe and Mr W.B. Edgeler, the proprietor of a chemist's shop, reflecting in 1899 on the changes to the town over half a century, recalled that there had been no Corn Exchange (the entertainments centre of the town in the late Victorian era), no bank, no hospital, very little in the way of schools, no gas, no reading room [library], no drainage, and, above all, no railway. Visitors to Petersfield had come by one of the many horse-drawn coach routes passing through the town such as the "Rocket", the "Nelson" or the "Hero".

In 1894, Petersfield was considerably enlarged by the addition of a large part of Sheet and a small part of Buriton parish. This geographical expansion, together with the concomitant rise in pupil numbers in the schools and the greater variety of activities run by voluntary bodies in the town, ensured the overall, growing prosperity of Petersfield at this time.

A bland announcement in the press the same year informed the public that the District Local Board proposed to re-name certain streets within the town. The six changes were to be:

New Way ... (to become) .... St. Peter's Road
Golden Ball Street .... Sussex Road
Horn Lane .... Heath Road
Chapel Street .... North Street
Back Lane .... Borough Road
Nine-post Lane .... Windsor Road

Not only did this come as a shock to the readers of the *Hants and Sussex News*, but the Board simultaneously announced its intention to remove the drinking fountain in the Square and to re-site it in the centre of the road at the bottom end of the High Street. The suddenness of the announcement inevitably led to some misgivings on the part of the public who vented their feelings in the following week's newspaper. This in turn led to a further debate by the Board at their next meeting, when letters of protest were read out, including one from the shopkeepers of Chapel Street; they won their case for the retention of the old name, as the road had been known as Chapel Street for such a long time. Another letter from a protestor complained that "Golden Ball Street" was a most appropriate name as it contained the historical interest of the old sign of a pawnbroker's business which had been conducted there years ago.

Chapel Street, Petersfield.

Chapel Street

Even one of the town's major architects, Mr H.T. Keates, objected to the abandonment of the old traditional names "in a place whose one claim to interest was that it was quaint and old-fashioned". One of the town's most respected doctors, Dr Brownfield, agreed with Mr Keates, adding that "the re-naming of the streets was the most unpopular thing ever suggested in Petersfield." Despite much discussion on the merits of each name change, Chapel Street was the only one to be retained, and the fountain remained in the Square. Sadly for the protesters, and perhaps also for future generations, some of the Board members' votes, which ultimately determined the new names, showed a majority of merely one or two votes out of a total of six votes cast. As to the suggestion that Station Road be renamed Winchester Road, the remark that they ought to consider the even older name of Cow Legs Lane was met with laughter; Station Road was kept.

About the time of the renaming of Nine Post Lane as Windsor Road, nearby roads were named Sandringham and Osborne to continue the royal theme – although Balmoral Way and (elsewhere in town) Buckingham Road were much later additions to the collection.

Annual events linked Petersfield to its predominantly agricultural community: August was the month for the highly popular Horticultural Show, begun in 1885 and held in a meadow adjoining Churcher's College; September brought the annual Horse Show, organised by the Fareham and Hants Farmers' Club, with its driving and jumping competitions; November saw the Autumn Show of farm and garden produce; since 1894, and in conjunction with the Horticultural Show later, there was a Home Arts and Industries Exhibition, with ten classes of prizes for articles of woodwork, basketwork, patchwork, needlework and carving.

The annual Horse Show

Agricultural matters

In the mid-Victorian period, it was the arrival of the railway in 1859 which had stimulated new growth in Petersfield, and the old rural industries, such as weaving, tended to diminish in importance. The Victorians had always considered that the land surrounding Petersfield was better suited to pasturage than to tillage. The sandy soil with an admixture of chalk from the Downs and clay from the Wealden bed allowed the growth of a quality of grass better adapted for cattle-grazing than any other part of Hampshire. Hence the high quality of milk produced in the local dairies, of which there were many in the town in the 1890s.

When three well-known farmers in the Petersfield area, meeting regularly at *The*

Dairy adverts in the Hants and Sussex News

Red Lion in 1892 to discuss their root crops – mangolds in particular – began to compete with each other over the merits of seeds deriving from Devon and those originating in Hampshire, the Autumn Show was born. Seedsmen from nationally known companies lent their support, Capt. the Hon. S.H. Jolliffe took the chair at the preliminary meeting and the first two-day event took place that autumn at the Drill Hall. Mr Cave presented a Silver Cup to be won annually and presented at a dinner at the end of the event. An annual fat stock show in the Square was also organised in 1902, but this was abandoned after six years.

However, notices in the press in 1893 announced that two local farms at West Harting and Steep were being sold by auction, together with all their livestock: working horses, heifers and steers, cows and calves, geese and poultry, bulls and pigs. The same year, the sale of valuable freehold building sites within Petersfield came onto the market, revealing the fact that the town was extending. The shift of emphasis from the town as a purely rural entity to that of a small suburban centre had begun.

In the later Edwardian period, there was still some sheep-shearing and hop-growing in and around the town and its villages, but even these were due to disappear in the inter-war years. The changes which came about in the agricultural community were due in part to recent inventions: tractors began to be used more and more and this reduced the need for intensive labour; bicycles allowed rural workers to seek

Hop-pickers

employment elsewhere, even to find work in the towns and cities; the days of the shire horse (for ploughing) were numbered as the ubiquitous Fordson tractor took over its role; scientific discoveries included a breakthrough treatment against blight and other similar rotting diseases, so that crop production increased and farmers' losses were reduced.

By and large, all rural workers were technically deemed to be "unskilled", there being little or no recognition of rural skills; it was therefore inevitable that, with the development of towns and new forms of labour in them, a new generation would leave the country and its squalid housing and working conditions.

The Petersfield Scrap Book

Over a period of about a year during 1892-3, the *Hants and Sussex News* published a regular series of articles entitled 'The Petersfield Scrap Book', written by its new editor, Frank Carpenter. Despite their often cursory historical references to the town in the nineteenth-century, the articles contain interesting nuggets of information on the old Borough of Petersfield, which had ceased to exist in 1885. Given the paucity of historical records on Victorian Petersfield (only one history of the town was published in that period – that by the Rev. J. Williams in 1857), these snippets serve as useful within-living-memory items by townsfolk of the time.

Churcher's College

At the time when this Scrap Book was being written, the town was beginning to see an increase in its housing stock, and a consequent rise in population. Among the more recent physical changes to the town were the new Churcher's College (1881), the Courthouse (1893) and the Post Office in the High Street (1892). Lavant Street, Charles Street and Chapel Street had also been built in the 1880s. While the population of the town had increased at a low rate since the beginning of the century (from 1,406 in 1801 to 2,294 in 1881, a rise of only 57%), in the next three decades it rose by over 60%.

Frank Carpenter, the newly appointed *Hants and Sussex News* editor, wrote in 1892 : "Of out of school hours, too, I have a very vivid recollection. I remember we used to go to Dark Hollow [the Carpenters lived in Oaklands Road] under the captaincy of George Palin, and dig out the sand until we had made quite a respectable cave. The entrance was only large enough to crawl through, but the interior would hold three or four of us, all more or less ambitious to become Dick Turpin or Jack Shepherd. Bell Hill copse, too, was a favourite playground. In the playground proper, rounders was certainly the most popular game; the balls we used were made by Miss Lambert, of rag and string, with a kind of netted covering and, when new and thrown swiftly, they left a good impression behind."

*The new Post Office
in the High Street*

Charles Street

Chapel Street

Lavant Street in the 1880s

On the subject of inn names in Petersfield, the following is an amusingly-concocted resumé of the inns which existed in Victorian times – probably also written by Frank Carpenter:

Frank Carpenter

and appoint the result.

The *Jolly Sailor*, hearing the *Five Bells*, rose with the *Sun* and walked into Petersfield to see the sights. He did homage to the *Crown* and saw the *Fighting Cocks*, the *Red Lion* and the *Golden Horse*, paying particular attention to the *Dolphin* and *White Hart*. He was much surprised to see a *Swan* close to the *Old Drum*, and trying to avoid the *Royal Oak* fell into the *Bricklayer's Arms*. He went into the *George* with the *Good Intent* of having one glass, but stayed in the *Market Inn* till the *Bell* struck eleven, when, supported by the *Volunteers' Arms*, he reached the *Railway Hotel*, where he dropped the *Blue Anchor* for the night, and went home with the *Coach and Horses* in the morning.

Education

Before 1870, education was not compulsory and, although a large variety of schools existed throughout the country for poor families, such as *Charity Schools*, *Church Schools*, *British Schools*, *National Schools*, *Dame Schools*, *Voluntary Schools*, *Sunday Schools* and even *Ragged Schools* (free, charity schools for destitute working-class children, later run by the Shaftesbury Society), their number was very small, and it was largely the privileged children of rich families who benefited from an education at a *Public* or *Grammar school*.

Petersfield had had its share of various types of school: apart from Churcher's College, which had been founded in College Street in 1729, a *National School* (Church of England) was built in Golden Ball Street [now Sussex Road] in 1837, a *British School* (Quaker), attached to the Congregational Church in College Street in 1845, and the *National Schools* (run by the Church) were opened by the Bishop of the Diocese in 1854. An *Infants' School* was added to these in 1859. However, there was at this time no one school which catered for all the children in Petersfield.

The early Victorian British School in College Street

The 1870 Elementary Education Act (the Forster Act) changed all this, and *Board Schools* were set up to provide classes which were compulsory for all children between the ages of 5 and 10, although some children could leave early in agricultural areas. They were run by School Boards, elected by the communities which they served; in Petersfield, the Chairman of the Petersfield School Board was John Bonham-Carter, a newly elected Hampshire County Councillor and the Chairman of its Technical Education Committee. The town required attendance at the *Board School* and parents who failed in their duty to do this were fined at the Magistrates' Court.

The two systems under which the Elementary Education of the country was carried on were the Board system and the Voluntary system. These two systems differed principally in their sources of income, the *Board Schools* dependent on the local rates (therefore secure), and the Voluntary Schools on voluntary subscriptions (variable and hence insecure). A further distinction was that religious instruction was given in the *Voluntary Schools* (according to the denomination of the provider) but not necessarily in the *Board Schools*. Since supporters of *Voluntary Schools* also paid their rates, they were paying twice over for the education of their children in these schools.

One school in the centre of Petersfield has been overlooked so far: Castle House School in the Square. Once known as "The Great House", this magnificent Tudor building had successively been the home of, among others, the Jolliffe, Bonham

Castle House School in the Square, c.1900

and Bonham-Carter families. When the latter moved to their new home at Adhurst St Mary in 1858, the building became a private school known as Castle House. It took its pupils (exclusively boys), aged between ten and sixteen, from a wide area and was run by the family of Edwin and Henry Stowe. Their successor was J. Arthur Perkin, who was Headmaster from 1889 until 1895. He was an old Carthusian, a great sportsman – he captained the town's football and cricket teams and had established the Golf Club – and he laid great emphasis on sport for his pupils. The school's sports days were held in the garden behind Castle House.

Unfortunately, when Mr Perkin left the town, there was no-one to take over the running of the school and, sadly, the building's contents were sold, including the school desks.

With the imminent rise in the school leaving age to 11 in the early 1890s, a heated debate was being conducted concerning the future educational provision for Petersfield. Current school buildings were so inadequate that new buildings were required with some urgency: places were needed for approximately 200 boys, 200 girls and 160 infants, but the Board Schools were only able to house two-thirds of these adequately. As a result, many schemes were proposed to meet the necessary requirements, including the construction of an entirely new school, preferably on one site. This policy was agreed, and new premises were proposed for the site between St. Peter's Road and Hylton Road where there would be sufficient space for infants, girls and boys in all "standards" (school years). There was a difficult interregnum during 1892 and 1893 when the younger Board School pupils

The Petersfield School Board School

were temporarily housed in the newly-acquired British School premises [in College Street, adjacent to the (then) Congregational Church and since demolished] and were managed by a Miss Boon with two assistant mistresses. By 1894, however, the new Board School was finally completed and all Petersfield children in the state education system would now being educated in the new building complex for almost a century to come.

It is extraordinary to discover just how many small private schools existed – and apparently thrived – concurrently with the town's Board School in the 1890s: Mr Avant's Preparatory School provided a "good commercial education for boys aged 7-14" and also taught music (organ, harmonium and pianoforte); Miss Henson's Ladies College at 24 High Street (run by Fanny and Susan Henson) offered "a

Miss Henson's School

Good Education, with careful attention to health and domestic comfort"; Miss Ball ran Petersfield Ladies' College in Ramshill and gave private lessons in "accomplishments and foreign languages"; Miss Lowin was the Principal of a preparatory Girls' High School where "superficiality is carefully avoided"; the strongly Methodist sisters Beatrice and Annie Richardson's school was situated in Sandringham Road; Miss Nixon's School was in Heath Road, and followed in the tradition of the P.N.E.U. (Parents' National Education Union, founded by Charlotte Mason to cater for home-educated children); Mrs Smith's Private School for Infants, taken over in 1894 by Miss Pescott, was in Lavant Street and taught English, writing, arithmetic and needlework; for twenty guineas per annum, the Misses Pink and Bull offered young ladies an education in English, composition, geography and history at Ramshill-House School; St. Laurence's Catholic church ran a school ("open to all") under Father J.I. Cummins and had about 30 children in the mid-1890s, but it closed in 1898. Few of the teachers in these schools were professionally trained, but the essential "three Rs" were taught and the strict discipline was generally tempered with kindness.

As to the question of corporal punishment in all schools nationally, the Chairman of the London School Board expressed the opinion that it

MISSES PINK & BULL,

RAMSHILL-HOUSE, PETERSFIELD.

Young Ladies

BOARDED AND INSTRUCTED IN ENGLISH, COMPOSITION, GEOGRAPHY AND HISTORY,

Ramshill-House School

was becoming easier to maintain discipline because the proportion of children who had not passed through infants' schools was declining. Early Victorian discipline, amply described by Dickens, for example, still only persisted among a few "waifs and strays" who had not been "broken in" by their teachers. By the later Victorian era, teachers who inflicted undue punishments on children could face a reprimand, a loss of part of their salary, a transfer to an inferior appointment, or, in extreme cases, dismissal.

Churcher's College had moved "up the hill" to Ramshill in 1881, thanks to the extremely generous donation of ten acres of land by Mr William Nicholson of Basing Park [now demolished] in Privett, who had purchased it from Magdalen College, Oxford. Just 34 boys, including 15 boarders, filled the space provided for three times that number, under their new Headmaster, the Rev. Giles Andrew. To fulfil the wishes of the school's founders, twelve scholarships were awarded to boys from the Borough of Petersfield. In 1893, a new Headmaster, the Rev. William Bond, was selected from a list of over 100 applicants and, three years later, pupil numbers had risen to 70, half of whom were boarders. The Council of Education designated Churcher's as a School of Science and Art; chemistry and physics were taught in newly-constructed laboratories and the pupils also studied carpentry and gardening.

W.G Nicholson, M.P.

Under Rev. Bond, Churcher's began more closely to resemble in character the larger and older-established independent public schools of the day, but, because of severe financial constraints, he was later obliged to accept aid from the local authority. He was not only responsible for the considerable expansion of Churcher's over a period of 26 years, but, as a councillor, he also participated widely in the life of the town. In this respect, his service to the school and town was matched by that of his woodwork and drawing-master, Norton Palmer, whose teaching tenure lasted for 35 years.

The school leaving age was raised to 11 in 1893, and to 12 in 1899. Petersfield's educational aspirations for its children extended to its adult population: in 1892, technical education classes were arranged for the Petersfield District in woodwork, cookery, horticulture and agricultural engineering to be held at various schools' premises. The object of these classes was not to train people to a high degree in technical fields, but simply to make them capable of turning their hand to any trade to which they might be put. At about this time, too, John Bonham-Carter announced that the travelling dairy of the British Dairy Farmers' Association would be visiting Petersfield to give a ten days' course in dairy farming.

In 1893, the "zealous and capable" Mr John Bonham-Carter proposed the setting up of a "Rural Polytechnic" in the town, with lectures on horticulture and sanitary science, thus complementing the recreational and instructional courses already available. To the previously offered subjects were added arithmetic, history, vocal music, drawing and shorthand; an advertisement for this new institution was published in the press in January 1894. Hampshire had been among the first few counties to introduce technical education to its citizens and their Director of Technical Instruction, Mr Vaughan Cornish, in explaining the objects of the scheme, quoted the Act of Parliament which had created the great London Polytechnic as aiming "to

Rev. W. Bond, Headmaster of Churcher's College, 1893-1919

Petersfield " Polytechnic " Committee.

EVENING CLASSES

FOR MEN AND BOYS,

Have Re-Opened for JANUARY, FEBRUARY AND MARCH, and will be held, as follows, in the

BOARD SCHOOLS, HYLTON ROAD.

ARITHMETIC AND HISTORY.—On Mondays, at 7.30, by Mr. J. D. MARSHALL & Mr. A. WALLER.

VOCAL MUSIC.——On Wednesdays, at 7.30, by Mr. A. WALLER.

DRAWING.—On Thursdays, at 7, by Mr. J. D. MARSHALL, (Art Certificate "D," South Kensington. There are only 6 more vacancies in this Class.

SHORTHAND.—On Fridays, at 7, by Mr. R. E. MARSHALL.

FEES—One Penny a Lecture. Boys under 14, may not enter unless they have passed the Elementary School.

The Committee and Teachers hope for a good attendance, each pupil endeavouring to take up at least two subjects; they may thus be encouraged to arrange for a continuance and extension of the Classes next winter.

J. A. PERKIN, Hon. Sec.

Advert for the new "Rural Polytechnic", 1894

promote the industrial skill, the general knowledge, the health and well-being of the working classes". Petersfield's Working Men's Institute, Athletic Club, St. John's Ambulance Brigade and the Literary and Debating Society all lent their active support to the new scheme, thereby enhancing its effectiveness in the cause of what became known as "continuing education".

By 1897, a series of evening continuation classes were being conducted in the Board Schools in botany, woodwork, physical drill (for both sexes), shorthand, bookkeeping, vocal music, drawing, history, domestic economy and needlework. The town had clearly made its mark in the field of education for all its citizens.

The Press

Petersfield's first local newspaper, *The Petersfield Weekly News*, had begun life in 1883, but it became the *Hants and Sussex News* in 1892 when the business was taken over by Mr A.W. Childs and the office and printworks were situated at the bottom of the High Street [now High Street Dental Centre]. Frank Carpenter was appointed its Editor at the age of 20; he had been a scholarship boy at Churcher's College from 1883 to 1886, after which he worked in various clerical jobs in the newspaper office, reporting on meetings and debates in the town until his appointment as Editor, a post he was to hold for the next 56 years.

Changing local press mastheads

The *Hants and Sussex News* was known far beyond the borders of Petersfield for its intelligent and literate reporting; for the cost of one penny, its eight pages covered not only local issues, but also national and international events in a seemingly random order. The front page consisted exclusively of large-format local adverts; pages 2 and 3 dealt with national news, including reports from Parliament; page 4 carried small advertisements from local businesses, while page 5 began local reporting in detail, with notes and comments on events in Petersfield and the surrounding villages and also reports on the cases heard at the Petty Sessions in the Magistrates' Court, held until 1893 in the old Town Hall in the Square, thereafter in the new custom-built Courthouse [now Petersfield Museum]. Page 6 reported on international events and page 7 consisted of literary extracts, either serialised stories or full-length articles with a literary bent. The back page carried general articles, often on agricultural or horticultural topics, articles aimed at women readers or reports of local societies' meetings and, later, a births, marriages and deaths column. There were also occasional supplements published.

The Old Town Hall in the Square

The newspaper therefore catered for a wide readership. There was no need for local residents to purchase a national newspaper to supplement the local news: local interests were comprehensively represented and reported and local businesses and private individuals enjoyed the support of "their" newspaper. As the 1890s progressed, more Letters to the Editor appeared in the paper, leading to real public debate on issues of immediate concern, and photographs started to feature towards the end of the century to support items with the greatest public interest.

With its expansion at the start of 1892 beyond the immediate neighbourhood of Petersfield, the paper saw itself as the representative publication for the districts of Liss, Liphook, Horndean, Havant, Emsworth, Westbourne, Hayling, Cosham and Waterlooville. It advertised its aims as devoting itself "to the honest and open discussion and ventilation of all questions affecting the district", and claimed to be "the most efficient advertising medium for this Eastern part of the county". It also promoted itself as "the only established and purely local organ for the East and South Hants Parliamentary Divisions, as well as those in West Sussex", thereby justifying its new title.

Cultural and leisure activities

With little spare time or money in the average worker's life for leisure, it was essential for people to find activities which were inexpensive, easy to access, and relatively spontaneous. Cycling seemed to fulfil these criteria and it was during the late Victorian period that both individuals and families took to the road by bicycle to explore their local countryside. In the 1880s, the Stanley safety bicycle came within the purchasing reach of ordinary farm workers, even those on low wages. The very popular Petersfield Cycling club had about 40 members in 1891. Since, previously, most country folk had remained largely in their own villages during their working lives, the bicycle became the means to broaden one's horizons, both literally and metaphorically. The High Street booksellers and stationers of J. Richardson produced a map of the area within a 20-mile radius of Petersfield for cycling and touring. Rowswell's cycle shop ("The East Hants Bicycle Depot") was doing such good business in the later nineties that it was able to move from College Street to more central premises in the High Street in 1899.

For the real enthusiast, there were cycling clubs waiting to organise tours and group activities. In Petersfield, The Old Drum became the stopping point of choice for members of the Cyclists' Touring Club. The CTC had originated in Yorkshire in the 1870s and, by 1883, had over 10,000 members. By the late 1890s, this number had risen to 45,000 and the Club had designed its own pub and hotel sign – the "winged wheels" –

CTC *Winged Wheel*

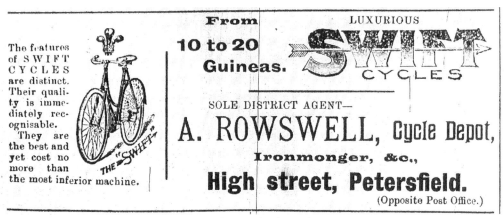

Rowswell's Cycle shop advert

to indicate and recommend places sympathetic to the needs of its membership. Nevertheless, even ten years later, it was clearly a struggle to overcome some of the natural impediments of the surrounding countryside: in his *Highways and Byways in Hampshire*, published in 1908, D.H. Moutray-Head writes that "nowhere are the Downs more irregular than by Petersfield, and the wildest jumble of wooded hillside, moorland, meadow, river valley, and wind-swept common, lies between the Rother basin and the headwaters of the Wey. Let none who wish to explore this country venture forth on a bicycle unless they be adepts at rough riding, have discovered an absolutely unpuncturable tyre, and have nerves of muscle to face any gradient that may suddenly present itself!"

The annual Heath Fair (the Taro Fair) which has always been held on 6th October, drew multitudes of people from Petersfield and the surrounding villages and a lengthy report appeared annually in the press on its success or otherwise (generally depending on the weather at the time). On the morning of the Fair, Mr Alfred Williams would conduct auctions of "useful cart horses and colts", being the working animals used by all farms in the neighbourhood, as well as "all classes of store sheep, beasts and horses". A successful Taro Fair would be one at which there had been a good supply of cattle, horses and sheep in the morning, and a large number of shows and booths in the afternoon and evening.

Britnell and Bramley cycle works

Local pride in the historic nature of the Heath Fair was emphasised by the *Hants & Sussex News* report which commented in 1893 on the fair "which, by the way, was granted to the Lord of the Manor as long ago as the reign of Henry III in the 13th century". The Cattle Fair that year had seen a noticeable decrease in the amount of stock brought in, and "everything was at a discount, sheep and beasts selling badly". The Pleasure Fair, however, compensated for this disappointment and "the country folk evidently still regard[ed]

The Taro Horse Fair

it as a grand institution". The attendance – made up of "the usual motley elements" – was high and "there was the usual hubbub on the ground, including a numerous collection of the inevitable gingerbread and toy stalls, rows of beer booths, coconut shies, knock-'em-downs, shooting galleries, swing boats, roundabouts, boxing booths, variety shows, cheapjacks (hawkers of dubious bargains), and the many other noisy appendages to a fair so full of vitality as the Heath Fair appears to be, when contrasted with the many extinct and decayed old fairs which have existed in the county." The most popular amusement was Bartlett's "admirable and richly adorned steam roundabout" which that year boasted "the exceedingly fine and novel effect of being lit up with *electricity* in the evening". The British Women's Temperance Association took advantage of the crowds at the Fair to welcome visitors to its refreshment tent and to circulate its literature, as did "the usual small group of religious tract distributors".

The major indoor venue in Petersfield for public entertainments was, until the opening of the Drill Hall in Dragon Street in 1899, the Corn Exchange. Built in 1866, this Italian-style building with its well-proportioned lantern roof, was effectively a simple, large, open hall to accommodate local cereal farmers conducting their transactions. However, since this market-place was only operational one day a fortnight, there was ample scope

The Taro Pleasure Fair

for other events to take place in the generous space inside. The Corn Exchange was an excellent venue for a huge variety of public meetings, rummage sales, concerts, plays, pantomimes, fencing and boxing displays, and even a circus. Clubs and societies also met there for their private functions: tableaux vivants, charity performances, lectures, parochial teas, or for prize-givings. Tableaux vivants were an art form beloved of the Victorians, consisting of static, costumed scenes, preceded by a short explanation of each before the curtain was raised.

It had also served as a County Courtroom, the Headquarters of one section of the Hampshire regiment of volunteers, and as a substitute for St. Peter's Church when the parish church was being refurbished by Sir Arthur Blomfield in 1873.

The Corn Exchange was the venue for "a form of amateur entertainment of which the public never seems to tire", a troupe of "Nigger Minstrels". The first appearance of such a group in 1900 drew in crowds and every seat was taken well before the performance started. The troupe performed on a large platform at one end of the hall "surrounded by pretty scenery and lit up by footlights

The High Street and Corn Exchange

and overhead gas jets" and gave "a fine selection of sentimental, plantation and comic songs". This type of entertainment – originating in early nineteenth century America and based on the songs, dances and dialects of African Americans – jumped the Atlantic to Victorian Britain, using "blacked-up" white actors and a traditional set of characters. Its successor even became a British light entertainment show called The Black and White Minstrel Show in the London theatre of the 1960s and on BBC TV until the late 1970s, after which it fell out of favour for its offensive and embarrassingly racist overtones and it was taken off air.

1894 marked the year in which tourism can be said to have started in Petersfield: the first trip in the first "char-a-banc" was advertised in the press by a "Local Tourists' Association" for a Thursday in July, leaving the town at 4.15 p.m. for Hindhead and the Devil's Punchbowl, taking in Hill Brow, Rake, Milland, and Liphook, and returning via Haslemere. Charabancs –

An early motorised charabanc

from the French *char à bancs*, meaning a carriage with (wooden) benches – were the earliest form of motor coaches; they were horse-drawn vehicles before the advent of petrol engines, and were popular with works' groups or organisations arranging trips to the country or the seaside for their employees or members.

The Tourists' Association must have been assailed by some clients who suspected they were making great profits from these innovative outings: in a letter to the press, the Association sought to reassure their clientele that they were neither a money-making concern, nor an exclusive or elitist organisation. They felt it necessary to justify their requirements for payment in advance ("the fares are fixed on the assumption that eighteen tickets will be taken") and that *"anyone* desiring a country drive might participate in the pleasure and advantage of excursions into the unknown recesses of the beautiful district surrounding Petersfield". They were keen to emphasise that there was no "rowdyism" on their vehicles, and that "while not unduly hilarious, [our trips] have always been cheerful and sociable".

An entertainment closer to home was afforded by the Heath Pond in 1895: boating had been proposed by some members of the public who expressed their regret and surprise that "there are no boats to be had for a quiet, restful, health-giving row or sail, where every natural facility exists". However, one of the two landowners, Lord Hylton, needed persuading of the merits of the case, and this may have influenced the members of the barely seven months-old Urban District Council who were clearly proceeding with great caution in the matter.

Skating was already permitted (the Pond froze over frequently in those days) as was bathing, within reasonable limits of time in the morning. There was some apprehension about opening up the Heath to this new activity, possibly because of a recent case, heard in the Petty Sessions, of gaming in a public place (on Petersfield Heath) on a Sunday afternoon, when a police constable had heard money being rattled by a ring of six men lying on the ground and calls for money to be put in the ring. The case was eventually dismissed. Perhaps, and more likely, it was the thought of the UDC's (and Lord Hylton's) income from a licence to trade in boating which swayed everyone's opinion: within a few months, the boatman, Mr J Aldred of Sheep Street, was advertising his two boats for hire that August. As the press commented:

The remarkable spectacle was afforded on Monday of a boat, with an experienced boatman in charge, plying for hire on the Heath Lake, and ... being freely patronised by a most appreciative body of people, notwithstanding the bad weather".

NOTICE! NOTICE!
___

To-morrow (Flower Show Day),
from 10 a.m. ;
And every evening after that day,
from 4 p.m.,

TWO BOATS

Will be on the LAKE ON PETERSFIELD HEATH, managed by an experienced Boatman, and anyone may enjoy a row round the beautiful lake, at 3d. per head.
___

The Boats are most comfortable and safe, and will carry six passengers each, and the Boatman will have the sole charge.
___

Family Parties can be privately arranged with for the use of the Boats at any time.
___

For particulars apply to the Boatman,

Mr. J. ALDRED,
Sheep Street,
or Mr. J. P. Blair, Chapel Street.

*First advert for Boats for Hire on the
Heath Lake*

By August, there were two boats for hire and, in September, there was even a fireworks display on the Pond from boats on a platform on the island.

A proposal to form a Town Band, initiated in the press in April 1896 by Mr C. Rawson of Lavant Street – the father of Admiral Sir Harry Lawson who became the Governor of New South Wales in the Edwardian period – led to a public meeting just one month later, where the idea was supported unanimously. Annual subscriptions and donations to the project were already underway,

The Heath, Pond and Music Hill in Edwardian times

and the band would be financially self-supporting. Their Bandmaster was to be a Mr A. Stacey, they recruited 14 members, and their instruments were purchased with the large amount of donations from the public. By July, they had procured blue uniforms for themselves and announced that they were open for engagements for flower shows and fetes.

The band also played regularly on Music Hill. This name originated from the natural mound and small amphitheatre on the north side of the Pond said to have been used for music played by French prisoners of war a century before, and, more recently, by the band of the Sheet Bridge Volunteers. It had also been an ideal vantage point for listening to the newly-installed eight-bell peal from St. Peter's in 1889, as a lyrical piece in the *Hants and Sussex News* reported:

> *"Anyone who has listened to the completed peal from Music Hill on a still evening will know something of the music which enchants the listener, and never fails to minister to his frame of mind, be he in want of sympathy or the companionship of joy".*

Starting in 1894, a November 5th Carnival took place in the town, ending on the Heath in the evening. It consisted of a parade of two brass bands, a score of floats from the town's traders, a decorated fire engine, participation by the cycling club, the illumination of Castle House, and a "guy" carried on a market hurdle.

Travelling menageries were popular in late Victorian times : in Petersfield, Mander's menagerie, one of the biggest on the road in the 19th century, pitched in

Mander's menagerie

the Square one Friday and Saturday in February 1898. That June, another nationally famous menagerie came to town: Bostock and Wombwell's "Royal Windsor Castle" visited the Square, and elicited the comment: "The collection of animals is a very excellent one; some of the specimens, notably the tigers, elephants and wolves, being exceptionally fine and the daring but graceful and effective performance with them revealed a pitch of training and mastery which it would be difficult to surpass."

The same year, Ginnett's circus, one of the oldest circus dynasties in Europe, set up its tent in a meadow near the station and a procession, "mainly representative of historic personages in glided cars or on horseback" paraded through the town and naturally attracted a large crowd of people.

However, such occasions not only represented a chance for children to see something educational, but also to witness an event probably as exciting as any, and one which would remain in children's memories for the rest of their lives. For example, it is quite possible that the thirteen-year old Fred Kimber had been influenced by these two travelling menageries; he was to develop his own menagerie in Tilmore Road in the early 20th century. But, as these travelling shows demonstrated, and as the residents of Petersfield later discovered, the night-time roaring of the lions and the screaming of the birds were not to everyone's taste or sensibilities!

Bostock and Wombwell's Menagerie

Nor was there any shortage of intellectual stimulation in the town. Indeed, the existence of the Petersfield Literary and Debating Society, founded by a young schoolmaster, James Parnell in 1884 when the Victorians' enthusiasm for public debate was at its peak, ensured that a wide variety of topics could be heard and discussed, from current local and national issues to more philosophical debates on religion and ethics, history and politics, science and the humanities. Meetings took place every week at the Town Hall under the Presidency of Mr W.B. Edgeler, a prominent figure in local politics. The Society had its own library which, long before the establishment of the "official" town library in 1926, served the community, alongside the other semi-exclusive libraries of the Working Men's Club and the Parish.

Local and National Politics

The composition of the Petersfield District Local Board, the elected body representing ratepayers which administered the affairs of the town before the emergence of the Urban District Council in 1895, had been a more or less static body of men. They were generally elected from within a small group of people consisting of, among others, Thomas Amey, J.P. Blair, W.C. Burley, Thomas Caparn, Rev F.J. Causton, Thomas Eames, W.B. Edgeler, Dr Brownfield, Dr Cross, H.T. Keates, Dr Leachman, A.J.C. Mackarness, Thomas Privett, Col. S.W. Seward and C.W. Talbot-Ponsonby. Several long-standing families had also featured largely in the conduct of the town's affairs, the most significant being the Bailey, Bonham-Carter, Budd, Burley, Eames, Gammon, Jolliffe, Luker and Mould families.

This group appeared to represent a fair cross-section of Petersfield society: doctors, shopkeepers, businessmen, churchmen, solicitors and landowners. From the time of its first Charter, Petersfield had always elected its Mayor at the Court Leet on the first Monday in Epiphany (i.e. in January). Coincidentally, the last Mayor of the old Borough of Petersfield (holding office for 21 years) before the Redistribution Act of 1895, which redefined the size of parliamentary constituencies according to population size, was Col. Seward, who died in December 1895.

In the general elections of the late Victorian period, the fortunes of the two major parties had fluctuated regularly, with their leaders Gladstone (Liberal) and The Marquess of Salisbury (Conservative and Unionist) alternating as Prime Minister until 1895, when the Conservatives remained in power for the next decade. Petersfield's M.P. was William Wickham (Unionist) both after the 1892 and 1895 General Elections, the former result being a win over the Liberal John Bonham-Carter, the latter being unopposed (the first uncontested Parliamentary Election held in Petersfield since 1866). In fact, the whole of Hampshire returned Conservative M.P.s in this period.

William Wickham, M.P.

At the local level, the political picture was changing with the newly formed Urban District Council (UDC) of 1894, whose area was to incorporate part of Buriton and

Sheet. The old Local Board, which had governed until then, had been composed of ratepayers' representatives; it had concerned itself primarily with river pollution, sewage disposal, surface drainage, and street watering and had operated under the name of the Petersfield Rural Sanitary Authority, although other Boards existed to serve other purposes: the Burial Board (to govern the cemetery); the Board of Guardians (to oversee the Workhouse); the Highway Board (principally preoccupied with the purchase of a new steamroller to improve road surfaces); and the School Board (to provide the administration of all the state schools in the town).

By all accounts, Petersfield residents were fascinated by this new electoral process; the press reported the scene at the count: "An increasing crowd was outside the Town Hall whilst this important operation was in progress, and beguiled the time of waiting by setting off a few crackers, indulging in a variety of hoaxes, and speculating as to the issue of the elections". Nine men were duly elected (out of a list of 14 candidates in total), with Mr W.B. Edgeler winning the most votes, with nearly 50 votes more than his nearest rival. The nine successful candidates were: Messrs Edgeler, Gander, Burley, Brownfield, Cross, Johnson, Durman, Amey and Crawter. Although women were eligible to present themselves as candidates at this election, none was forthcoming. The new body was elected for a period of three years.

The fortnightly meetings of both the Urban District Council and Rural District Council (which replaced the old Highway Board and Sanitary Board) were reported regularly in the press.

Lyndum House

At a meeting called at the Town Hall by Mr J. P. Blair in 1896, which was attended by nearly 70 ratepayers, he proposed that the town purchase Lyndum House as a most suitable site for the UDC to meet in: commodious accommodation for the Council Offices, ample space to accommodate a future Town Library and storage space at the rear for a horse and cart and the water cart. Since there was much debate at this time over the future of the market in the Square, mainly as a result of the insanitary conditions which prevailed there, Mr Edgeler suggested that the market might also be removed to the field behind Lyndum House. Mr Blair's motion was carried unanimously.

Unfortunately, unbeknown to those present at the meeting, the property had already changed hands that morning when a deal on Lyndum House had been concluded with a private buyer in London.

The Temperance Movement, campaigning against drunkenness and excess and, more rarely, for total abstinence from alcohol, had originated as a mass movement in the early years of the Victorian era. Its equivalent for younger age groups was the Band of Hope, founded in 1847, to save the children of the working classes from the perils of drink. The Petersfield Branch of the Band of Hope had been founded in 1872. Both movements had their supporters in Petersfield in the 1880s

The Petersfield Band of Hope

and 1890s. Speakers like Miss Agnes Weston from Bath, the founder of the Sailor's Rest Institutions which tried to combat alcoholism among sailors in Temperance hostels, toured the country seeking support for her movement. In 1896, together with representatives from all the town's churches, Miss Weston and her colleague and business partner, Miss Wintz, attended a conference in the Town Hall, then moved to a public meeting in the Corn Exchange, where a great temperance crusade was launched, aimed at creating a union of all Temperance Societies and workers in East Hampshire.

The Temperance Hotel in the Square on market day

It was natural that the Temperance Movement should find its strongest support among churchgoers, but it also appealed, for both practical and philosophical reasons, to the emerging Women's Suffrage movement. At a public meeting in Petersfield Town Hall in 1892, there had been a gathering of the British Women's Temperance Association, at which the main speaker was Mrs Boys, of

Dumpford, a staunch advocate in Petersfield of Temperance principles. The town's suffragist sympathisers were numerous and vocal. Many meetings were held in the town, outside speakers came to lecture, and there was a fervent local response to the contemporary demands for votes for women.

New buildings in the town

Major additions to the townscape of Petersfield in the last decade of the Victorian era included those of St. Laurence's Catholic Church (1890), the High Street Post Office (1892), the Magistrates Courthouse (1893), and the Connaught Drill Hall (1899).

In 1885, the wealthy family of Laurence Trent Cave had settled in the Petersfield area, where they bought the Ditcham estate. Sadly, Ditcham House itself was destroyed by fire in 1888, but it was rebuilt within a year. Next, Mr Cave bought an acre of land in Station Road and had St. Laurence's built there in 1890; at its opening, a Mass was celebrated by the Bishop of Portsmouth, the Rt. Rev. John Virtue. Although at first the church was served by clergymen from France, this responsibility was taken over by the Benedictine Monastery of St. Laurence at Ampleforth in Yorkshire, whose monks were of the English Benedictine Order. The Rt. Rev. J.I. Cummins, writing in the *Ampleforth Journal* in 1896, remarked that "Petersfield might claim a notice in the *Ampleforth Journal* as being the only mission in the Laurentian *Familia*

dedicated to the Patron of the mother monastery – a distinction it owes not to the devotion of any of S. Laurence's sons, but to the fact of its founder being a namesake of that saint." The whole cost of St. Laurence's, built in the Italian style of architecture, was defrayed by Cave himself, who was received into the Catholic Church two years later.

Petersfield, R. C. Church.

St. *Laurence's Catholic Church*

The new Post Office of 1892, situated next to the old Dolphin Inn at the end of the High Street, was designed by H.T. Keates, the Petersfield architect, whose design was the one selected from among the five bidders; the work was financed privately by Mr John Butterfield and built by the firm of William Mould of Dragon Street. The ground floor of the new building was designated for the various departments of the Post Office, while the first and second floors became the official residence of the Postmaster. This building served as Petersfield's main Post Office until 1922, when the present office was constructed in the Square.

Petersfield thus benefited from a bespoke new building for its Post Office, the previous ones having moved several times in the Victorian era, the most recent one sharing the property at no. 34 High Street on the opposite corner [now the High Street Dental Centre]. Not only could the public have a better service in the new office, but it could also enjoy the improved delivery service by its postmen: a third postman was recruited, a second delivery at 10 o'clock instigated, and collections at the station were to be more numerous, enabling postings to be made there up to 9.50 p.m.

H.T. Keates' Post Office, 1892

Plans for a new Magistrates' Courthouse had been drawn up by the County surveyor, Mr James Robinson, and the building, to be situated on spare land behind the Police Station, was opened for business in January 1893, with sessions to take place every Wednesday. [This is the building now occupied by the town Museum].

It consisted of a courtroom, with accommodation for the Justices, Clerks, police and witnesses, the press and members of the public. There were also two more private rooms: a J.Ps' (Justices of the Peace) consulting room and a female witnesses' waiting room. In previous years, Magistrates' Court proceedings had been held in the Town Hall in the Square, and the County Court sat in the Corn Exchange; the new building provided well-heated and more comfortable surroundings for all, a great improvement on the Court House at Havant or any of the other courts in the county. The Stuart coat of arms – believed to be royal, but in fact the arms of Charles FitzRoy, Earl of Southampton – which had hung in the old Town Hall in the Square, was later renovated and re-hung behind the Bench in the new building in 1904.

The Court House accommodated three different kinds of court: the Petty Sessions, the County Court and the Coroner's Court. The Petty

The Magistrates Courthouse, 1893

Sessions were held weekly in front of either two or three magistrates, and cases were reported in detail in the local press. They dealt with offences which would incur a maximum of three months' imprisonment. In the late Victorian era, these consisted mainly of cases such as assault, drunkenness, begging, vagrancy, sleeping rough, theft, failure to send children to school, poaching, "hard swearing", stealing ferret and rabbit nets, and defrauding the railway company.

The County Court was held at intervals, when a circuit judge would hear minor civil cases; the Coroner's Court existed for cases of unexpected deaths, when a local jury would also be summoned to attend.

The new Drill Hall of the "I" Company 3rd Volunteer Brigade of the Hampshire Regiment in Dragon Street, was opened in January 1899. It was a conversion of the old malthouse of the brewery on the site, which had belonged to the Chichester brewing family of Henty's in the early Victorian period. The architect was, again, H.T. Keates and the builder, Gammons. Inside, the upper floor was removed and a new roof constructed, while outside, space was allocated for a parade ground. Facing Dragon Street, a newly constructed building housed the Sergeant's house, with an attempt being made to provide it with a bold military character by adopting a castellated style with 15th century details. Entrance gates were constructed from oak beams salvaged from the old malthouse. Both the house and the gates have since been demolished.

Original entrance to the Drill Hall, Dragon Street

Over 600 people attended the opening ceremony and saw the hall draped with flags, lit by incandescent gas, and with a platform at the east end for notable guests; at the opposite end was a gallery from which the Regimental Band of Portsmouth gave an opening concert. This was an inspiringly patriotic day for Petersfield and for the 120 men of the regiment who looked forward to increasing their recruitment as a result of their new Headquarters. The Drill Hall was soon to serve as the premier venue in the town for many types of public events, which previously had been staged in the Corn Exchange. It provided sufficient space for exhibitions, concerts, sports tournaments and, from 1911 until 1935, served as the major concert hall for the Petersfield Musical Festival.

The new Drill Hall, 1899

As for residential expansion, many terraces were added to the housing stock of the town, including Jubilee Terrace in Windsor Road, North Road, and the north side of Station Road, all built in the late 1880s. Large private villas were also being built for the wealthier residents in various parts of the town.

The Laurels, Station Road

North Road

Station Road, north side

Weston Road

One interesting development took place at this time: the establishment of a Petersfield Women's Institute in November 1900 to match the Working Men's Institute which had been in operation since 1886. No new building took place, as the new Institute took over the offices of the *Hants and Sussex News* at the end of the High Street. This building had had a chequered history, being the premises of various types of shop in the 18th and 19th centuries, then, in 1878 the town's Post Office, until that moved to its new building across the road in 1892, since when it had housed A.W. Childs, the well-known printer's, stationer's and owners of the local newspaper. When, in his turn, Mr Childs removed to 21-23 High Street, the property was purchased by another businessman, Mr William Rickard, who leased part of the building to the incipient Women's Institute.

The space available in their new home provided the women with reading and recreation rooms, a tea room and a music room. It opened in the evenings until 10 p.m. and charged a membership of ten shillings a year. Its first president was the Hon. Mrs Kathleen Lyttleton, wife of the Bishop of Southampton who resided at Castle House in the Square, and the Secretary was Miss Ethel Pickering, who remained in post for the next 25 years. Ethel and her sister Emily were by now well-established photographers in the town who had opened their studio in Lavant Street in 1898.

The Hants and Sussex News offices, High Street

In 1893, a certain Joseph Boismaison, of Lavant Street, proposed that the town find "with a very small outlay, a nice room" to constitute its first museum. This idea gained some support, including that of Lord Hylton and Mr Wickham, MP, but unfortunately it foundered upon the same type of negativity which has always seemed to permeate certain bodies and individuals within the town; one supporter explained the phenomenon in a letter to the press: "the prosperity of the place depends somewhat upon certain of the inhabitants working more in harmony with the others, and setting aside their petty jealousies instead of, as at the present time, endeavouring to throw obstacles in the way of everything that is brought forward for the benefit of the Town, unless it happens to be brought forward by themselves". The Museum proposal got no further and the town waited a further century for the wish to be realised.

Queen Victoria's Diamond Jubilee

On 23 September 1896, Queen Victoria surpassed King George III as the longest-reigning monarch in British history. The Queen requested that any special celebrations be delayed until 1897, to coincide with her Diamond Jubilee which was made a Festival of the British Empire at the suggestion of the Colonial Secretary, Joseph Chamberlain.

In Petersfield, an initial suggestion for the commemoration of the Jubilee was to name the Council's imminent new hospital "The Victoria Isolation Hospital". Despite seeming attractive as a proposition, however, the Council preferred to provide Petersfield with the hospital independently of the commemoration. Further suggestions from the public included a new public clock; town festivities and entertainment; the renaming of the Heath "Victoria Park"; improvements to the Square (and removing the cattle market to an area near the station); the planting of trees and shrubs around the statue of William; a beacon fire on Butser (in answer to a national call for this); a footpath around the Heath; a public hall (to be named the Jubilee Memorial Hall); the planting of 60 trees in one street or in clumps "to beautify the town and preserve that character of rusticity which was essential to its prosperity";

Queen Victoria's Diamond Jubilee celebrations

the addition of a free wing to the Cottage Hospital; a Jubilee Medal for each child in the town; a new clock for St. Peter's church tower; a Volunteer Drill Hall and general assembly room; a new laundry for the Cottage Hospital (and the renaming of the building as the Victoria Cottage Hospital); the provision of a public bath; and a drinking fountain.

The three suggestions which found most favour were the new town clock, a Public Hall and help for the Cottage Hospital; a committee of twenty men, consisting of the nine members of the UDC with a further eleven invited, was set up to debate the issue the following week. At this subsequent "somewhat lukewarm" meeting, there was no very general pronouncement in favour of any one scheme. The Cottage Hospital extension carried the most votes, while the Public Hall – or, more precisely, a piece of ground in the town on which to build "a nice ornamental building, such

as was very much wanted in Petersfield, for lectures or anything of that sort, and council offices" – attracted those who predicted (correctly) that Lord Hylton was willing to pull down the old Town Hall and the adjoining cottages in front of the church.

The Cottage Hospital had been built by public subscription in 1871; it housed 37 patients in its first year, but this number had risen to 87 by 1896 and its funds were running low, so a financial injection would have been seen as

The Cottage Hospital

a life-saving measure in more senses than one. Fewer than half its patients came from the town itself. Nevertheless, the hospital received the general approval for a special "nest egg" to mark the Jubilee, but only after over half the sum collected was spent on a day of children's festivities.

When the time came, in June 1897, to commemorate the Jubilee in Petersfield, the language of the press mirrored the people's feelings with its outburst of "truest rejoicing and most fervent enthusiasm worldwide in extent" which accompanied its reports of the events of June 1897. In its own homily to the Queen, the *Hants and Sussex News* was no exception to this rule:

> *In commemorating good Queen Victoria's 60 years of gracious and beneficent sovereignty over these realms, her millions of faithful subjects, irrespective of race, creed or colour, in every corner of the vast and mighty Empire on which somewhere the sun is always shining and the growth of which has been such a marked feature of the present reign, will in countless ways and by varied means testify their admiration, affection and loyalty, with a sincerity and significance the like of which has never yet been equalled in the records of the world.*

In acknowledging the achievements of the Victorian era over which the Queen had presided, mention was made of "the striking expansion of Britain; the dispersion of the race over the surface of the globe; the social amelioration of the people; and the enormous and unprecedented progress in science, art, literature and commerce". A 250 page book, entitled "Queen Victoria and her people" by the Rev. C.S. Dawe, was published for the occasion, detailing the personal and political events in her lifetime, the social and scientific progress achieved, and ending with a homily to "Our Noble Queen".

*"Queen Victoria and her People",
published 1897*

As part of the Jubilee celebrations in Petersfield, a programme of sports was arranged, open to all residents in the UDC area. This included running races for children and adults, a tug-of-war, putting the weight, a 1 mile cycle race, "climbing the greasy pole for a leg of mutton", a wheelbarrow race (blindfold), a 100 yards veterans race (for the over 50s) and a Volunteers Race (500 yards) in full marching order, firing and returning over hurdles. Prizes were given to the first three winners. The day of celebration, on 22nd June, began, under "the most propitious climatic conditions", with church bells being rung at intervals throughout the morning (with 60 volleys to complete the peals); an old people's dinner (for 130 men and women) in the Corn Exchange at midday; a presentation to all children in the Board Schools in the afternoon, followed by a procession along the High Street to the Heath. The procession consisted of a detachment of Volunteers, the Town Band, a specially-designed, flower-bedecked symbolic "royal" pony-cart bearing children dressed as a Queen with maids and

Celebrations in the Square for the Jubilee

grooms, followed by marching children with flags and two church Drum and Fife bands. They processed to the cricket ground, dismissed, and the Athletic Sports began. In the evening, services of thanksgiving for "Accession Day" were held in all the town's churches. The schools were closed all the following week.

Sanitation problems

Petersfield was prone to serious flooding in the 1890s and this affected not only the inhabitants of the central part of the town, but also had a deleterious effect on the running of the market in the Square.

The south stream, running parallel to, and south of, Borough Road and Hylton Road near the Forebridge (the crossing point at Dragon Street and Hylton and Sussex Roads) frequently flooded after thunderstorms and the occupants of houses in Sussex Road were extremely vulnerable, due to a blockage in the stream.

At the other end of the town, the inhabitants of Rushes Road suffered the same fate whenever the nearby Drum Stream overflowed. The land bordering the Drum River behind the first houses in Winchester Road used to be known as Potters Flood and John Bridle, who was brought up in Rushes Road in the Edwardian period, recounted in his Memoirs how he once saw his father's boots floating down the stream after a flood.

The Drum River frequently flooded nearer the town centre, even causing problems in Chapel Street, because there was no adequate dispersal of surface water at that point. The Old Drum Inn was badly affected by this flooding and Miss Amey, the owner of Amey's brewery in Frenchman's Road, complained of bad odours from local manholes. Mr H.T. Keates, the town's Sanitary Surveyor and Inspector of Nuisances, was often called upon by the UDC to effect repairs to the drainage and to unblock the streams. The Great Storm of 7th September 1899, which was recorded as the worst in living memory, led to the following report in the *Hants and Sussex News*:

> *The downpour of rain was tremendous and the water rushed down the streets in enormous volumes so that everywhere floods soon became general and vast quantities of grit and stones were washed out of the roads. The drains became choked; in fact, no drain would be equal to such a perfect deluge as the Petersfield drains were required to cope with, and in several places where the manholes of the main sewers were under water, the contents of the sewer bubbled up into the roadways.*

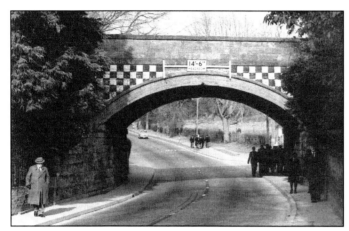

Ramshill railway bridge

Houses, shops and inns were flooded, under the railway arch [then at the bottom of Ramshill] the axles of sheltering carts were covered, water ran into the backs of houses on the north side of Lavant Street and the ground floor of the Old Drum Inn was immersed, as were the cellars of shops in Chapel Street. The subway at the station was converted into a swimming bath and the rails were under water, such that the Station Master, Mr Chandler, employed the Midhurst train to ferry passengers from one line to the other, to avoid the porters having to carry them across singly! The town's fire engine was used non-stop from 5 p.m. to 9 p.m. pumping out water from Chapel Street cellars at the rate of 180 gallons per minute. In Sheep Street during the storm, two large rats, probably driven from a cellar by the water, ran down the street and one was caught and killed by a dog in the back yard of a house.

The following year, the UDC agreed that the flooding which the town had experienced was a disgrace and reflected badly on the Council. It was agreed that a loan should be obtained to widen the streams in their entirety and to purchase a filtration system which would ensure that flooding did not occur again. Meanwhile, the Medical Officer of Health, Dr Leachman, reported that he had been obliged to condemn the water from the Drill Hall well as unfit for public consumption.

In 1900, the UDC purchased a new water cart to cleanse the town's streets; it had a capacity of 400 gallons and was fitted with a patent revolving distributor. This measure was vital not only to ensure the cleanliness of the streets – and to prevent ladies' dresses becoming intolerably dirty along the pavements – but also to clear away any subsidiary rubbish caused by the market in the Square. Complaints were already being expressed by the public and stallholders at the market over the poor, even insanitary, state of the area and the owner of the land, Lord Hylton, was asked on more than one occasion to carry out improvements.

A Victorian water cart

Indeed, the whole ownership of the Square was also in question and Lord Hylton asked whether the UDC would be willing to undertake control of the Square and all the accompanying market rights. This became something of a political hot potato, as the town's charter specifically guaranteed the holding of a market and the Council would not envisage losing their centuries-old political right. It was resolved to ask Lord Hylton what price he wanted for the charter. As it happened, he died in 1899 and therefore did not survive to see the transfer, which finally took place on 1st January 1903.

The town Fire Brigade

The Petersfield Voluntary Fire Brigade was formed in September 1889 by invitation of the Lighting Inspectors. Twenty officers and men made up the brigade, but there were mercifully very few fires reported in the first few years of its existence. The engine and equipment – hand-operated water pumps, a hose cart and a separate wheeled escape ladder – were housed in a small building in New Way [now the public toilet in St. Peter's Road]. For each call-out, horses were hired privately and the funds for this were raised by public subscription. Water was obtained from ponds or streams.

Marjorie Lunt and Mary Ray have written:

> The alarm to call the town fire engine was raised by a bell

Petersfield Fire Brigade 1893
Captain W P Jacobs   Deputy Captain C Hoar

The Fire Brigade, 1893

fixed to a tall chimney on the old Corn Exchange; it was activated by pulling a rope attached to it, which, at its lower end, was fixed to the wall and enclosed by a glass panel which required breaking. Whoever summoned the fire engine was obliged to wait until a policeman arrived to take the address of the fire. Someone else would have to go to fetch the horses needed to pull the engine; these were owned by Mr Terry in Dragon Street and were also employed to pull hearses. (PAHS Bulletin, Autumn 1984)

Within a month of the Brigade's formation, there was a fire at a local farm, where a hayrick had to be extinguished. However, fires were few and far between: in the whole of 1897, for example, there were only three calls out and one of these was a false alarm.

A fire broke out in the West tower of St. Peter's Church in September 1899. At about 9 p.m., smoke was seen pouring through the openings of the belfry and a glare came from behind the window. The fire brigade, under Captain W.P. Jacobs turned out quickly but had difficulty in reaching the fire as the tower staircase could not be used and there was some delay in getting some sufficiently long ladders to scale the tower. Luckily, the fire was extinguished after an hour: it had damaged the belfry floor and roof, and the clock had stopped. The only damage to the interior of the church was by falling debris and water. (Mary Ray, ibidem)

The cause of this fire was never discovered.

In 1904, the original horse-drawn fire engine was replaced by a Shand Mason Steam Fire Engine (popularly known as a "steamer"). To create steam power to drive the pumps, a fire had to be lit under the boiler first, thus causing severe delays in getting to any fires.

Petersfield's new "steamer"

In 1906, the parish councils of Harting, Rogate, Bramshott and Hawkley each agreed to contribute ten shillings towards the cost of an electricity connection between the Post Office and the Fire Station. The local firemen had electric warning bells fitted in their homes and, in addition, there were blue enamelled signs with the word "Fireman" affixed to their houses. (Mary Ray, ibidem).

The Union Workhouse

Petersfield's Workhouse at the end of Love Lane, dating from 1835, continued to serve its purpose throughout the Victorian and Edwardian eras. It housed, on average, between 50 and 60 inmates during this period and offered accommodation and meals to the aged, the destitute, and homeless and workless men, women and children. At times, there were almost as many tramps who sought temporary

The old Union Workhouse

relief there, but this was a passing, itinerant population which fluctuated according to the seasons. The Workhouse was run by a Master and Matron and overseen by a Board of Guardians, elected by the local council and numbering 16 men and women. The Chairman of the Board of Guardians in the 1890s was C.W. Talbot-Ponsonby.

The institution regularly asked for, and received, donations of money, help in kind, and charity on special occasions. In the summer, for instance, it appealed for funds to enable the inmates to be taken on a day's outing to the seaside. As an advertisement explained: "It is the one red-letter day in the year for those who, through no fault of their own, have been obliged to accept the refuge of the Workhouse". At Christmas, offers of food were sought, and there were always sufficient amounts donated for a traditional meal to be enjoyed by all the inmates; a public collection of funds enabled 40 boxes of coal to be bought for needy families in the town, including the Workhouse. At New Year, entertainment was organised for the inmates, and volunteers came to the Workhouse to give of their time and services.

In 1898, sanction was sought by the Rev. F.J. Causton of St. Peter's Church to build a chapel for the Workhouse inmates; this was followed by a public appeal for £400 to fund the project, with the Rev. Causton himself donating the first sum. Rev. Causton, who had celebrated his silver wedding anniversary in 1899, had been at St. Peter's for 13 years and was held in high regard by his parishioners. The money was

The Workhouse Chapel

raised, the building was designed by the architect to the Guardians, H.T. Keates, was completed by Gammon and Son a year later, and officially dedicated by the Bishop of Southampton in 1900.

The railway level crossing

In 1897, in correspondence with the Petersfield U.D.C. on the matter of the difficulties encountered by vehicles at the level crossing in the town, the London and South Western Railway declared that :

> The detention of public vehicles at the level crossing between the hours of 8 a.m. and 7.30 p.m. [showed] the average number of vehicles ...was only 50, the average length of stoppage 2 minutes 14 seconds, and the length of time the gates were closed each day averaged only 1 hour, 4 minutes and 5 seconds. This company [considers] that the grievance of the inhabitants is one of sentiment only and that there is no reasonable cause for complaint.

To the request by the UDC that "the Company erect a bridge or a tunnel, because the crossing is a continual source of annoyance and danger to the inhabitants", the railway company replied that either a bridge or a tunnel were impracticable and unnecessary. In fact, a study by the Board of Trade showed that the surface of the roadway in a tunnel would be only 6

The level crossing with the main and Midhurst branch lines

inches above the water table of the adjoining stream at that point; it was therefore quite out of the question that a tunnel could ever be constructed there.

The Town Clerk commented that he considered the crossing a most dangerous one, and that horses were often frightened by trains whizzing by. The Council agreed that they should ask the Member of Parliament to take the matter up with the Railway Company.

No changes were made to the crossing for vehicles; the iron footbridge for pedestrians was, however, completed and opened in August 1897.

The future of the market

The so-called perennial "market trouble" came "as regularly as swine fever and should receive the same drastic treatment", according to an "agricultural correspondent" in the press in 1897. The primary objections to the market were said to be its insufficient space; its insanitary condition; and its danger to human life. It was an open secret that the Ministry of Agriculture was only awaiting a good opportunity to condemn the condition of the market. Furthermore, the writer stated, "Where else would horse-dealers be allowed to give exhibitions at full speed among a crowd, or cattle-salesmen to turn down horned stock to empty drapery stores and fill hospitals?"

The cattle market

In brief, the suggestion was made that an alternative site be found for the cattle market which would allow the proper facilities to be provided – i.e. sanitary conditions for the public, safe conditions for the animals and adequate space for both public and animals. Five possible sites were mooted: the Heath (difficult ownership question); meadowland in Hylton Road near the gasworks (low, wet and remote); some land opposite the Railway Hotel (inadequate area); a meadow behind the Volunteer Arms (wrong side of the railway); and meadowland north of Station Road, between Tilmore Road and the Midhurst branch line (undoubtedly the best site).

A steam tractor

This conflict of interests had also been exacerbated by the problem of access for the various groups who required the Square: during itinerant shows which took place on a Sunday, for example, a traction engine was puffing away and stands were being erected just as people were arriving for a church service; on a Saturday evening, the fish business caused the greatest sanitary hazard of the week; clothes, machinery and food stalls all vied for space in a higgledy-piggledy fashion within a very confined area.

However, the decisions taken soon afterwards by the two major landowners in 1898 were to have far-reaching implications for the town and these will be discussed in the next chapter.

The Isolation Hospital

In 1893, there was an outbreak of scarlet fever in Petersfield and around the district; it was brought to the attention of the Local Government Board shortly after this that there was no provision for the isolation of infectious cases in the town.

A Committee was rapidly set up in 1897 to administer the future hospital, but, unfortunately, delays and political prevarication put back its provision. Finally, the Hampshire County Council applied to build it in 1899 and, at the subsequent enquiry held in the new Petersfield Courthouse, there was no opposition of any kind to the project. In fact, land had already been earmarked and purchased at "Sandy Lane" (the popularly used name for Durford Road) for the building. However, by 1900, the hospital was still not completed and scarlet fever broke out again that year.

The building was finally completed in 1901, but not without an initial shock: within months, it had had a narrow escape from a devastating fire which broke out one night at about 10 p.m. when a disinfecting chamber overheated. The caretaker, Mr West, called the Fire Brigade just in time to save further damage.

The hospital [now the site of Home Way] provided beds and cots for up to 27 adults and children during the Edwardian period. It finally closed in 1948 and became a long-stay geriatric care centre named "Heathside".

The Boer Wars

The Boer Wars was the name given to the South African Wars of 1880-1 and 1899-1902 which were fought between the British Empire and the descendants of the Dutch settlers – the Boers (farmers) – in the independent republics of the Orange Free State and the Transvaal in South Africa. The rebellion against British rule in the Transvaal in the first war had led to William Gladstone granting the Boers self-government.

The Second Boer war was lengthier than the first, involving large numbers of troops from many British possessions overseas and ending with the conversion of the Boer Republics into British colonies, later forming part of the Union of South Africa. In Britain, the action in South Africa was strongly opposed by many leading Liberal politicians and most of the Independent Labour Party as an example of the worst excesses of imperialism.

In Petersfield, by contrast, there was a large attendance in the Corn Exchange at a meeting in aid of the sufferers of the (second) war in December 1899. Patriotism was to the fore, a lantern slide show illustrated scenes taken in South Africa by a former resident there, and the sentiments expressed in speeches were greeted with outbursts of cheering.

In early January 1900, Captain Percy Seward, commander of the Petersfield Company of the 3rd Hants Regiment, was selected to command a company of equal numbers of men from all five battalions of the Hampshire Volunteers, a total of around 120 men altogether. They began their training at Winchester and were expected to embark for South Africa at the end of January.

Detachment of the "I" Co. 3rd (D.C.O.) V.B. Hants Regt. off to the War.

Photo by   G. West & Son, Gosport.
Standing—Private W. Budd, Private Knowles, Private Money, Private Boniface, Private Wills, Private C. Budd.
Sitting—Private Browning, Captain Seward, Colour-Sergeant Gosling.

Captain Seward and a Petersfield detachment off to the Boer War, January 1900

The first ever "live news" picture to be printed in the *Hants and Sussex News* (as opposed to a studio photograph) appeared that month, showing the Petersfield detachment of the Hampshire Volunteers due to go off to the war. Captain Seward, in the centre of the picture, is surrounded by his colour-sergeant and seven privates. After receiving their inoculation against typhoid fever, they were due to proceed to musketry training at Gosport until their embarkation.

There was a stirring scene for their departure from Petersfield Station shortly after 7 a.m. on 17th January, which had been preceded by a march from the Drill Hall accompanied by the Buriton Brass Band, the St. Peter's Drum and Fife Band, and the Fire Brigade, all in uniform. A great crowd had followed them to the station, many shops were lit up and the Gas Company had arranged for full street lighting on their route. Songs were sung along the way, cheering broke out occasionally, many flags were draped from houses and shops, and the Union Jack flew from St. Peter's church tower.

In the dark, "wretchedly wet and cold" morning, and through the steam from the engine, Mr Bonham-Carter addressed the detachment, offering the town's congratulations and farewell. The final "hurrah" was a surprise farewell from the railwaymen who had placed fog signals on the line which exploded as the locomotive steamed away.

It was four months later, in May, that the Relief of Mafeking was announced and, as the press reported, "not only in Petersfield itself but in all the villages round, people gave expression to their exultation at the triumphant issue of the splendid defence which for seven long months Colonel Baden-Powell and his courageous handful of 'sons of the Empire' had maintained in the face of unparalleled dangers". Amidst all the celebrations in the town, the statue of William III underwent an amusing transformation: he was clad in a khaki helmet with a windmill of red, white and blue feathers on the top and a khaki-coloured mantle over his shoulders. A Union Jack was suspended around his outstretched hand, and another round his horse's neck. The following Thursday, the Queen's birthday and the relief of Mafeking were celebrated together with a children's parade through the town and sports on the Heath. All Petersfield children were invited to attend and bring with them a Union Jack.

Interestingly, that August, the cyclists among the Hampshire Volunteer Regiment introduced a novelty in the history of the Volunteers Corps by the formation of a Baden-Powell Club. They were anxious to improve their knowledge of the art of scouting, as set down in Baden-Powell's recent publication "Hints on Scouting".

MAFEKING RELIEF.

REJOICING AT PETERSFIELD.

Petersfield shared in the thanksgiving and rejoicing which took place throughout the country and empire on Saturday, on receipt of the long desired news of the relief of Mafeking, in a manner befitting the great occasion. As the event to be celebrated possessed features which appealed to the imagination and hearts of the people even more strongly than those connected with the relief of other towns besieged during the war, so the outburst of patriotic sentiment, pride and gratitude with which the glorious tidings were hailed was more spontaneous, more hearty and more widely diffused than at the celebration of any of the moving incidents which have attended the war hitherto. This, indeed, seems to have been the case everywhere, and not only in Petersfield itself, but in all the villages round, people gave expression to their exultation at the triumphant issue of the splendid defence which for seven long months Colonel Baden-Powell and his courageous handful of "sons of the empire" has maintained in the face of unparalleled dangers.

The Relief of Mafeking, 1900 – press report

It was, of course, this book which inspired many such groups and which led in a few short years to the Boy Scout Movement throughout the country.

Early closing

The question of whether to institute early closing times or days had been debated over a number of years from 1892: it had even led to the formation of an Early Closing Committee under Dr Leachman's Chairmanship. The committee decided almost unanimously to adopt an early closing time of 4 p.m. on Thursdays and this came into effect in April 1892. It was barely eighteen months later that this was extended to limiting shop opening hours to 7 p.m. on four days a week. However, this measure did meet with opposition from some traders, who felt that it was "detrimental to business and inconvenient to customers" and closing time was changed to 8 p.m.

Dr Leachman's comments at a public meeting in 1899 to discuss the issue further reveal much about the lives of the Victorians: when he had come to Petersfield [in the 1870s], "nobody dreamt of taking a holiday themselves or giving it to others. The shops used to open at half past seven or earlier, and the shutters were not put up until half past nine at night, and on Saturdays not until eleven. Now everyone recognised that every worker had a right to a certain amount of leisure, in which he could exercise and develop those faculties of body and mind which were not called into operation in the ordinary round of business." The ensuing proposal to close shops at 2 p.m. on a Thursday was, however, left for further consideration later.

It was a sign of these changing times and the demand for greater free time for the working man – and shopkeepers in particular – that such measures were being introduced. New shops were opening in the town – five opened in Chapel Street, and some private houses in Lavant Street were also

New shops in Lavant Street in the 1890s

being transformed into shops, including a new photographic studio belonging to the Misses Pickering, who, for many years, were to produce many memorable pictures both for private use and public sale. Another newcomer – in 1900 – was the firm of W.J. Fuller, the family grocer, provision merchant, baker and confectioner, who was to remain in "London House" [on the corner of Lavant street, now Petersfield Photographic] for half a century. The erstwhile aspect of middle class residential respectability presented by Lavant Street was disappearing fast as the commercial interests of the town began to transform and dominate this street barely fifteen years old.

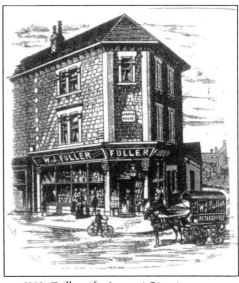

W.J. Fuller, the Lavant Street grocers

This end-of-the-century craving for a more favourable work-life balance was exemplified by the simultaneous extension of leisure activities available to all. It was in 1895, for example, that the first Petersfield Dramatic Society was formed, instigated by a Mr W.H. Kneller. This Society put on a farce and a drama at the Corn Exchange at Christmas that year. It marked the beginning of Petersfield's long and extensive association with the performing arts, soon to be enhanced by its own Musical

Festival at the very start of the new century.

Street lighting

A frequently recurring theme featuring on the agendas of the old Local Board and, later, the Urban District Council, was that of the public lighting of Petersfield's streets. Throughout the Victorian

Gas lamps in the High Street

era, the town had been very poorly lit and, in 1889, tenders were invited for gas or oil lights to be installed. Ninety gas lights were eventually supplied by the Petersfield Gas Company, costing £2.8/- per lamp per annum, effecting a considerable improvement on the previously gloomy aspect of the town.

However, ten years later, the dilemma of a choice between gas and the (new) electric lighting systems occupied much of the Council's debating time. An investigation into the pros and cons of electric lighting produced the result that few people were prepared to have their rates increased to pay for the required electricity supply and it was condemned as "an extravagance and a luxury". Councillor W.C. Burley added to the argument by stating that they were "upon the eve of having a very great improvement in gas lighting", referring to the new technology of the Welsbach incandescent gas burners which, by virtue of their use of mantles to produce a brighter light, were being installed in many European and North American towns at the end of the nineteenth century.

After the ratepayers were petitioned on the matter and a public meeting held in the Corn Exchange, the UDC opted (by five votes to three) for a provisional electric lighting order. This, however, took another twenty years to materialise and Petersfield had to tolerate its gas lighting until the early 1920s.

Society Marriages

The relatively small number of prominent people involved in the town's affairs in the closing years of the nineteenth century were no longer from the traditional aristocracy – the erstwhile lords of the manor – but those from a background in what was loosely (and patronisingly) called "trade". They were the products of large Victorian families and their associated Victorian work ethic, which ensured their survival over many generations and were destined to guarantee the reputation of the family name. When two such families were brought together by marriage, their combined status and commercial power benefited both their families and the town as a whole.

In 1899, two such marriages took place within a few months: William Luker, the eldest son of Robert Luker, the co-owner with his brother William of Petersfield Brewery in College Street, married Florence Helen Seward, the youngest daughter of Samuel Seward, the last Mayor of the Borough of Petersfield and the owner of the large farm at Weston

William Luker   Florence Helen Seward

The Luker–Seward marriage, 1899

known for its hops. The ensuing partnership was celebrated as "this happy alliance between two such well-known and highly esteemed families". Their fourth child and third daughter, Betty (later Betty Wardle), described her Luker grandfather's brewery as "very much a family affair", while her Seward grandfather "made sure that his family took an active part in local affairs."

The second of these local alliances was that between Edward Talbot-Ponsonby, the eldest son of C.W. Talbot-Ponsonby of Langrish House, and Marion Nicholson, the youngest daughter of William Nicholson of Basing Park, Petersfield's M.P. who served twice as Petersfield's M.P., first as a Liberal, then as a Conservative after the Liberal and Unionist merger of 1912. This was described as "a matrimonial alliance between two of the leading families of this part of the county [which] could not fail to excite wide public interest, the respective fathers [being] both influential and highly respected men".

Deaths

In the closing years of the nineteenth century, the deaths of four town notables occurred: Colonel S.W. Seward, as we have seen, had been the last Mayor of the old Borough of Petersfield for 21 years, and his death in 1895 broke the link with Petersfield's Victorian era in a most poignant way. The Seward family had lived at Weston for almost a century; Col. Seward was highly respected among the local community for his active part in the governance of Petersfield, as a member of the 3rd Hants Volunteers, and as a successful agriculturist and hop-grower.

The following year brought the death of another long-serving councillor, the popular and influential Thomas Amey, who was one of the largest employers of labour in the district. Originally a farmer from Steep, he turned to dairy farming at his Rushes, Borough and West Mark Farms and acquired great notoriety – and wealth – for his "milk powder" product. In the late 1870s, he turned his attention to the brewing trade and opened his Borough Brewery close to the station [where Littlejohn now stands], where he had his own private siding for the delivery of barley and other supplies. He served the town as a Poor Law Guardian and as a member of the Local Board, then the Urban District Council. He had a very large family and his five daughters survived him, Elizabeth taking over the running of the brewery and expanding it after his death.

Petersfield's M.P., Mr William Wickham, died in 1897. He was a lawyer, a J.P., deputy lieutenant for Hampshire, and vice-chairman of the Hampshire County Council. He first entered parliament as a Conservative in 1892 and was re-elected unopposed in the 1895 General Election. His sudden death two years later caused a bye-election which brought in another Conservative, Mr W.G. Nicholson, the eldest son of William Nicholson of Basing Park, a former Conservative M.P. for Petersfield, after an extremely close contest ("long to be remembered as the fiercest parliamentary fight" Petersfield had known) with the Liberal, Mr John Bonham-Carter.

Undoubtedly the most significant loss to Petersfield, however, was the death at the age of 70 of Lord Hylton in 1899. His father had been the Rt. Hon. William George Hylton Jolliffe, for 24 years the M.P. for Petersfield who had been raised to the peerage (as Lord Hylton) in 1866. Lord Hylton was Lord of the Manor and one of the largest owners of property in the town; he had entered the army at the age of 20 and served in the 4th Light Dragoons in the Crimea and at Sebastopol; his first constituency as a Conservative M.P. was Wells, in Somerset, which was passed on to his son in 1895. Although he had withdrawn from public office in the early 1890s, his life revolved around the family seats at Ammerdown Park, near Bath, and at Merstham House in Surrey, with which the Jolliffe family had been associated for four generations. It was his brother, the Hon. S.H. Jolliffe, who retained Lord Hylton's previous connection with Petersfield. He lived in the peer's old residence of Heath House, thus keeping the Jolliffe association with the town. Lord Hylton had made only infrequent visits to Petersfield in recent years, but did actively support the Petersfield Volunteers, had founded the Working Men's Institute, and often met the wishes of the townsfolk in matters affecting the improvement of the town.

-oOo-

CHAPTER 2

1898

Two nineteenth century prints of Petersfield held in the Hampshire Record Office depict the Market Square viewed from the north. The first, an engraving by H. Bond from a drawing by T.H. Shepherd, shows the south and east sides of the Square, with a small number of cattle and some sheep pens, a horse-drawn coach, and a few desultory farmers and onlookers.

Petersfield Market Square by T.H. Shepherd

The date is not specified, but it must represent the scene at some time between 1812 (when William III's statue was re-erected in the Square) and 1859 (when the railway came to Petersfield and horse-drawn carriages had been superseded). It is more like a representational sketch than an accurate architectural or realistic drawing of life in Petersfield's central marketplace.

The second illustration, on the other hand, drawn by Armytage and Crew, has a clearly defined and animated crowd of besmocked farmers attending to their livestock and, in the background, gaggles of top-hatted gentlemen apparently examining the larger cattle displayed along the south side of the market square.

The Market Square by Armytage and Crew

In both prints, however, the most interesting part of the view for the modern reader is the presence of the three substantial buildings standing in front of St. Peter's Church. From east to west, they are: the old Petersfield Town Hall, built by Colonel Jolliffe in 1828 and housing both the Borough (and, later, the Urban District) Council chamber and

Petersfield Magistrates' Court; the offices of the *Hampshire Post*; and the elegant Queen Anne style former Pince's School, latterly an auctioneer's offices. These last two buildings also formed the focal point of a third drawing, owned by The Petersfield Society, which was used to portray "Old Petersfield" in lantern slide shows in the late 1940s. Here, the north door of St. Peter's can be seen through the passageway leading below the first floor offices of the *Hampshire Post*.

"Old Petersfield" (lantern slide)

North side of the Square, pre-1898

Three rare early photographs of Petersfield Square taken in the early 1890s show more details of these buildings: the complete row of buildings on the south side of the Square; the Town Hall and the newspaper building with a passageway through to St. Peter's; and a photograph by the Petersfield photographer, J.P. Blair, depicting what appear to be four schoolboys in the foreground outside their school, Castle House, in the north-west corner of the Square.

Petersfield in the 1890s was a busy place. The population of the town had begun to rise rapidly at the end of the nineteenth century, by 17% (from 2786 to 3265), for example, between 1891 and 1901. The imminent developments in the Square in 1898, therefore, together with proposals the same year for a takeover of control of the Square from a private owner (Lord Hylton) to public ownership (the Urban District Council) suggest a desire for rationalisation and expansion in the private, public and commercial sectors. These changes also indicate the presence of a sizeable group of wealthy residents and entrepreneurs among the population. New shops were built along Chapel Street (Lavant Street had been completed ten years earlier); electricity came to the town (forty years after gas had been installed); with flooding and drainage problems throughout the town, a better water supply system was being contemplated; the Petersfield School Board in St. Peter's Road was opened in 1894 [the Senior School for boys and girls is now the Infants' School and the Infants' section is St. Peter's Court]; plans were drawn up for a new electric laundry in Sandringham Road; and several fine villas were being

The Hampshire *Post passageway to St. Peter's*

constructed throughout the town, notably at the top end of Chapel Street.

Queen Victoria's Diamond Jubilee in 1897 had been marked not only in a vigorous spirit of celebration, but also by a desire for ostentatious private and commercial building renewal. This led to the announcement in October 1897 of a "generous offer by Lord Hylton and Mr W. Nicholson" [William Nicholson of Basing House, Froxfield, Petersfield's M.P.], made at the fortnightly meeting of the Urban District Council. The *Hants and Sussex News* carried a report on the proceedings, indicating that it was the intention of these two major landowners in Petersfield to improve the Square by handing over to the Council the houses belonging to them in front of the church, between the Market Inn and Mr Wright's house [now Rhona Russell] "on condition that they pulled them down and undertook to complete the improvement by laying out the site and forever keeping it as an open space".

The vice-chairman of the Council, Mr R.G. Cross, declared that it would be an immense improvement, adding that "there might be one or two people who would think otherwise and say that it was pretty to see the old church peeping over the roofs of the houses", but he had recently been inside some of these houses and, "from a sanitary point of view, the sooner they were demolished the better".

The Square from the north-west corner

The UDC Chairman, Mr W.B. Edgeler, J.P., agreed, but said that he was not quite so clear as to whether an open space would be as nice looking, unless some ornamental building were erected in the middle, but "they could not judge of that until the houses had been pulled down". It appears from the Council Minutes that they had been seeking to bring about this "improvement" for several years. Of the eight members of the Council present at this meeting, only one voice, that of Dr H.M. Brownfield, the well-known College Street doctor, raised any objection. He said that "putting aside the sanitary consideration, the houses formed one of the most picturesque parts of the town" and that the decision to demolish the buildings would be a most unpopular move. Mr H. Gander felt that simply throwing open the graveyard would not be an improvement. However, not for the first (nor the last) time in such affairs, money played its role: Mr Cross thought that "if it cost £200 to pull the houses down, it would be money well spent", and, with the Chairman and Vice-Chairman in agreement over the demolition, the meeting concluded with the resolution "that the unanimous thanks of the council be presented to Lord Hylton and Mr Nicholson for their gifts, and that the council undertake to pull down the buildings, and afterwards consult the donors' wishes as to laying out the ground as an open space."

A certain amount of doubt about the situation seemed to creep into the following Council Meeting in November, when a letter received from Lord Hylton indicated that he was ready to pull down his buildings (the Town Hall and some cottages at the rear), but that he would not do so until he had the consent of Mr Nicholson to pull down his property. In addition, he had decided not to hand over the site to the Council. Dr. Brownfield remarked (tartly, no doubt!) that the Council had thanked Lord Hylton for something he had not offered! He added that he had made up his mind to protest most strongly at spending "one farthing of ratepayers' money" on the scheme; he was sure that if a public meeting were held, or a poll taken, the majority of ratepayers would be against the proposed demolition. After Mr H.T. Crawter and Mr W.C. Burley, neither of whom had been at the previous meeting, had spoken – the one to suggest that the cleared site be used as an extension of the Market Place, the other that after the demolition by the owners themselves, the site be handed over to the Town Council as trustees – the subject was dropped.

Brief reports of little substance emanated from the Council's deliberations in the *Hants and Sussex News* during the next few months, except for the announcement, in March 1898, that Lord Hylton was prepared to bear the whole cost of the demolition of all three properties, and to build a wall and create a paved open space in their place.

By April 1898, the demolition of the properties had started. Under the headline "The Market Square – generous concessions to the town", the report spoke of the matter being the subject of negotiations between the owners and the Urban District Council "for several months past". Conceding that not everyone might be in agreement with "the wisdom of the undertaking", it reiterated the gratitude the town should feel towards the generosity of his lordship and Mr Nicholson in removing the buildings and preserving the site as an open space, "which so many people anticipate will be a great public improvement". The report concluded thus:

True, it will involve the destruction of one of the most picturesque bits of old Petersfield, including the curious goggle-eyed windows immediately in front of the entrance to the church from the Square, and this fact has considerably exercised the minds of a few who regard that as the chief consideration. But most people will agree that the prime merit of the undertaking will be to fully expose to view the grand old fabric of St. Peter's, which has so long been hidden behind these buildings, and to remove structures which are not particularly calculated to assist sanitation, and some of which have been in a very dilapidated condition for a long time. A few weeks, therefore, will see an enormous alteration in the Square, and though, as we have already hinted, there are those who doubt the necessity or advantage of the action now being taken, we are sure the town as a body must feel much indebted to the gentlemen by whose kindness and endeavours it has been brought about. The removal of the old Town Hall, which has been a very useful meeting place, and which is surrounded by not a few interesting memories of the town and its history during the present century, was viewed with some anxiety, but with his characteristic good nature Lord Hylton, immediately he became aware of the loss which it would be to several societies, kindly undertook to provide other accommodation, and thus laid the town under a further debt of gratitude to himself. The Town Hall will probably be the last of the buildings to come down. The start has been made upon the cottages at the rear.

Press comment on the 1898 demolition

In fact, the Town Hall was the first of the buildings to be demolished, the arched stone colonnade of its front façade being preserved and re-erected, to be subsequently used, first as a storage space for hurdles (used on market days to form pens for sheep and other livestock), then as part of a gentlemen's toilet, later collapsing into a derelict and shabby relic of past glories, but, finally, being recently resurrected and restored as Cloisters Café.

    In the three months following the removal of the properties in the Square, the press reported on Lord Hylton's proposal to build a wall on the site of the foundations of the old cottages, to be constructed of the old materials and faced with stone and coping of old tiles, and to rehang the present gates on new piers. This is the church wall we see today. He further proposed to take the Town Hall colonnade and place it with a flat roof seven or eight feet out from Mr Wright's house, which would have the effect of breaking the blank wall of that house. However, the colonnade was eventually placed at the other end of the gap, as we can now witness, and we are thus left with the tall blank wall of what used to be known as Square House, for many years the Commercial Hotel [and now, Rhona Russell].

So what did Petersfield lose as a result of these machinations? First, one fine eighteenth century and two nineteenth century buildings at the heart of the town; secondly, an elegant passageway opening out onto St. Peter's Church; and thirdly, a central Town Hall-cum-meeting place for many of the town's societies. But what perhaps represented an equally great, but more moral, loss was that of the almost covert nature of the deliberations between the Council and (primarily) Lord Hylton, whose hold on the town was in any case beginning to wane. This "development" was to be the swan-song of the Jolliffe family in Petersfield – the first Lord Hylton died in October 1899 and his eldest son, Captain the Hon. S.H. Jolliffe, died in South Africa the following year. The Hylton family sold their rights to the market to the UDC in 1902 and the estate was finally auctioned off in 1911, thus ending the Jolliffe family's connection with the town after almost exactly two centuries. What clearly characterised these deliberations over the Square were, first, an extreme deference by the Urban District Council to two of the town's three wealthy and substantial landowners (the third being John Bonham-Carter); secondly, a demonstration of the power of a very small body of men over the affairs of the town; and thirdly, the complete absence of any attempt at gauging public opinion or of airing the Council's deliberations in the local press. It was not until after the Second World War that the town's business was conducted in a more democratic and transparent way and that interested parties and pressure groups made their arguments felt over particular issues.

–oOo–

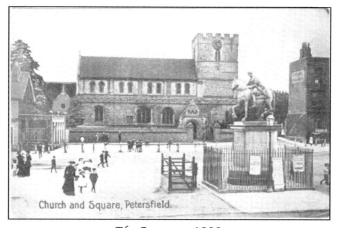

Church and Square, Petersfield.

The Square c. 1900

CHAPTER 3

The Death of Queen Victoria

Following a custom which she had maintained throughout her widowhood, Queen Victoria spent the Christmas of 1900 at Osborne House on the Isle of Wight. Rheumatism in her legs and a fall down some stairs at Windsor had rendered her lame, and her eyesight was clouded by cataracts. Throughout January, she felt weak and drowsy and her mind was confused. She died on Tuesday 22 January 1901 at half past six in the evening, at the age of 81.

In 1897, she had written instructions for her funeral, which was to be military as befitting a soldier's daughter and the head of the army, and white was to be worn in preference to black. Her funeral was held on Saturday 2 February in St. George's Chapel, Windsor Castle, and, after two days of lying-in-state, she was interred beside Prince Albert in Frogmore Mausoleum at Windsor Great Park.

Queen Victoria was the longest-lived British monarch (unless and until she is surpassed by Elizabeth II), and reigned for a total of 63 years, 7 months and 2 days, making her the longest-reigning British monarch and the longest-reigning Queen regnant in world history. When she died, her successor, Edward VII, was already 59 years old.

In Petersfield, the *Hants and Sussex News* expressed the nation's grief in a black-bordered report :

THE

Hants and Sussex News,

PETERSFIELD, JANUARY 23, 1901.

QUEEN VICTORIA DEAD.

The mournful news which we publish in another column, and which reached us as we were going to Press last evening, will excite a national grief without parallel and cause a sense of loss in every individual soul in the land which cannot be expressed in words. Victoria, our beloved Queen, beyond compare the most illustrious, great and good of any sovereign the world has ever seen, has paid the debt of Nature. after lingering between life and death for several days, and has passed to her rest amid a manifestation of profound sorrow and veneration never before witnessed. The long and glorious life which has been the pride of the empire and wrought such unutterable good to so many generations has ended at last, and we are dumbfounded at the thought. But at such a time hearts are too weighed down to be able to express the aching feelings which arise or to adequately describe the irreparable loss we all so deeply feel. This only may be said, that the measure of our grief is the measure of our affection, and that it is surely true that Britain, and Greater Britain beyond the seas, will need all the strength and courage possible to go forward into the future without the noble Monarch who has for so many years been the one example above all others that has produced all that is best and most worthy in Englishmen and women the world over. The new century has dawned darkly for us, but the influence of the departed Queen will illumine all the years to come and inspire her subjects and their descendants to follow the exalted rule of life which she set and maintained through the 63 years which saw her throned Queen of these realms and true mother of her people.

It was natural that most social events were cancelled that week: flags were flown at half-mast, church bells were muffled and the local Petersfield press described how "the people very generally donned some symbol of mourning, whilst every tradesman and many of the licensed victuallers shaded their business premises in some way, either by black shutters or otherwise". In some neighbouring parishes, the news was not known until the following morning. On Buriton church tower, the flag and mast were carried away by a fierce gale which raged that night. By order of the Earl Marshal of England, public mourning properly commenced within a few days and in Petersfield, as elsewhere, it was quite rare to see people in the street not wearing some sign of mourning; black dress was very commonly worn.

Mourning was even more evident on the day of the Queen's funeral, when her coffin was taken by ship to Portsmouth, then by train through Fareham and Havant along the south coast line to Victoria and thence to Windsor, to lie in state. The inclement weather added to the sense of grief – cold, heavy rain persisted throughout the day – and, with shops and public houses closed all day, most private residences had their blinds drawn as a mark of respect. "The town wore a most depressing and deserted appearance" as people passed through the streets to attend one of the numerous memorial services. St. Peter's Church had its flag at half mast, and, by the

start of the service at noon, the church was already full. Public bodies such as the "I" Company Hants Regiment and the Fire Brigade were represented, the clergy wore black stoles and the congregation was one mass of black, with the mourning accentuated by black drapings round the pillars in the nave.

Throughout Britain, of course, such memorial services were held in every parish. It was a time of great mourning and of an historic event to be marked; it was also a time to reflect on monarchy itself and the lecture by J.H. Badley of Bedales at the Literary and Debating Society's meeting a week later, tuned in closely with this sentiment. Entitled "Patriotism", and considered to be one of the most admirable lectures the Society had heard, it specifically dealt with the possibilities of teaching patriotism. Aware of the delicate nature of the subject in the recent and present climate, Badley spoke of the questions (or what might be termed problems) of Empire, ones that our children would have to solve. Quoting Tolstoy on the subject, he rejected the Russian's notion that patriotism, far from leading to noble sentiments, created a debasement of society by enhancing the position of

An illustration from "Queen Victoria and her people"

From a photo.   Russell & Sons.

those in power and enslaving those who are its victims. Badley, quoting the Boers, claimed that their patriotism had been the sign of vigour and vitality in a nation, and the lack of it the sign of decay and dissolution. In every school, he argued, as in every home, our aim should be to create a model Empire and love of country was only love of home on a grander scale.

Badley's discourse reflected an intellectual's approach to contemporary events: a respect for, and an understanding of, the concept of monarchy; a simultaneous pride in, and questioning of, the recent Boer wars and the role and importance of education in society's approach to these intangibles.

Victoria's reign had seen prodigious progress in the material prosperity of her people. The Edwardian era at the start of the new century found itself embroiled in more than mere shifts in wealth, however: social deference, technological change, population growth, local politics and its limits all brought their own controversies and a need for some difficult decision-making.

-oOo-

CHAPTER 4

The Edwardian Era

Introduction

S tatistically, the fraction 1/3 creeps into the social fabric during the Edwardian
period, illustrating the transformation of Britain since mid-Victorian times.
Whereas two thirds of the population had lived in small towns and villages
in 1871, by 1901 two thirds now lived in cities, and London was the largest city in
the world. Less than a third of the population had the vote (i.e. 2/3 of men and no
women) at this time. In 1901, nearly one third of women had regular jobs, mainly
in manufacturing – overwhelmingly in the textile industry in the north of England.

Key factors in the economy were the preponderance of working-class women now
in domestic service as the middle-classes grew in prosperity. Women's emerging
emancipation both politically and economically produced the Woman's Suffrage
movement. Public transport flourished with the introduction of omnibuses and
motor taxis and there was, naturally, a correspondingly massive reduction in the
number of horse-drawn vehicles on the roads.

C.F.G. Masterman's *The Condition of England*, published in 1909, highlighted the
disparities of wealth and opportunities among the various social classes. By the
end of the Edwardian decade, only 8% of the workforce worked on the land. The
Britain of 1910 belonged more and more to the middle class residents of the cities
and suburbs who were increasingly challenging the right of the landed aristocracy
to run the country.

We might reasonably talk of the many revolutions that took place in Edwardian
times. Of these, the technological was the most visible – in public and private
transport; in balloon and airship development; in telephones; and in powered flight,
with the Wright brothers' inaugural success in 1903 and Bleriot's cross-Channel
flight in 1909. Edward VII's own preoccupation with motoring as recreation probably
stimulated this trend, as did his renowned pursuit of pleasure. The Victorians'
modest respectability had given way to the Edwardians' lavish hedonism.

An educational revolution was occurring slowly but surely: Balfour's Education
Act of 1902 aroused deep passions and was opposed by the Methodists and other
non-conformists who saw the measure as a surreptitious way of providing taxpayer-
financed subsidies for Church of England Schools. It abolished the old Victorian

School Boards and brought in Local Education Authorities to organise school funding, employ teachers and allocate school places. The 1908 Children's Act or "Children's Charter" was designed to prevent the exploitation of the young; it made child neglect a criminal offence. Borstals, instituted the previous year, had ensured that minors were no longer housed in adult jails.

The multi-faceted social revolution of this period was exemplified by the Licensing Bill of 1908, reducing the number of pubs (a measure which itself had grown out of the Victorians' pursuit of temperance); the so-called "People's Budget" of 1909, which shifted the rates of income tax, the tariffs on tobacco and spirits, death duties and estate duties to benefit the poorest in society; and the Pensions Act of 1908, which assisted the elderly on low incomes.

If there was a Spirit of the Age, it was probably the growing awareness of the inequalities in society: the Conservative electoral débâcle of 1906, when a Liberal landslide brought two decades of Conservative rule to an end, reflected this new consciousness and signalled the beginning of a social revolution which had been waiting to happen. Poverty, as a major social problem, needed to be addressed. The self-consciously new Edwardian era was to witness a marked shift in social and political emphasis over the next decade, with the slow demise of the phenomenon of "noblesse oblige" and, in smaller communities like that of Petersfield, the gradual abandonment of the so-called "squirearchy".

The ambience of Petersfield in Edwardian times has been well summarised in the Petersfield Historical Society's Monograph, High Street, Petersfield:

> At the beginning of this [20th] century, the High Street was still a centre of activity. Along the pavements walked tradesmen and business men, servant maids doing the shopping, children with their nannies, nursemaids pushing perambulators, and ladies wearing hats and gloves, their long dresses held up out of the dirt. Along the street came horse-drawn vans and carts, and bicycles ridden by messenger boys, postmen and policemen. Very occasionally, a motor car or taxi-cab could be seen taking people to The Dolphin Hotel or The Red Lion or to private residences.

From the memories of pre-First World War Petersfield by elderly residents recorded in the 1970s, we learn that there was a lady who walked all the way from Froxfield to sell butter at 1/- a pound if customers gave a regular order. Mrs Bennetts of Oaklea in Station Road remembered hearing the clip-clop of horses in the street and the milkman bringing the milk in cans and measuring it into customers' own milk jugs. Mr Stanley Johnson's father was a "family grocer" in Sussex Road, who supplied groceries and game to local families. The Johnsons also purchased pheasants from Colonel Nicholson of Basing Park, whose wife regularly drove to Petersfield in her trap. People also bought hares and rabbits from Col. Bonham-Carter at Buriton and venison from Uppark.

Characters in the town recalled by residents who were children in the Edwardian era included "Darkie Lucas" who lived in a caravan in Durford Road and had a barrel organ; Jim Daughtry the "rag-and-bone man" who lived in Swan Street and drove his pony and cart around the town calling out "Any old rabbit skins?"; Fred Kimber and his exotic menagerie in Tilmore Road; Old Jack Rider from *The Fighting Cocks* lodging house who sold bunches of watercress in the town, crying his wares wherever he went; "Birdie" who sold small songbirds, such as linnets, which he caught on the Heath and kept in a large bag; Sam Hardy, an old Harrovian who moved to The Spain in 1907 and bought no. 2 when the Hylton Estate was sold in 1911, was known for his connection with the Hambledon Hounds and for driving his horse-drawn carriage around Petersfield while singing the songs of Harry Lauder; and Georgie Cox who did the round of the farms washing cows for three shillings and sixpence per farm.

From these accounts, it is easy to imagine our small town as one existing in a bygone age, when individuals stood out as more or less eccentric characters, who pursued their menial trades as best they could; with hindsight, it is equally easy to imagine the larger picture of a town in transition, moving from the individual, the everyday, the humdrum and the poverty-stricken, to a larger community governed by the wider forces of (unequal) prosperity, social change and material progress.

Front page of the Hants and Sussex News, 1st May 1901

The Coronation of Edward VII

In order to consider what steps should be taken in Petersfield to commemorate the Coronation, a public meeting was called in April 1902 by the Chairman of the UDC, Mr R.G. Cross, at which he sought approval from the public for a proposal already unanimously agreed by the UDC. This proposal took the form of a public subscription towards building a new Town Hall. In addition, there was to be a general entertainment on the Heath on the day of the Coronation, consisting of a tea for all and athletic sports and amusements for young and old.

Edward VII *and Queen Alexandra, as illustrated in the Hants and Sussex News*

As regards the possible site for the Town Hall, land had already been provisionally purchased for £700 in Heath Road between the Working Men's Institute [now the Scout Hut] and the "Red Lion" buildings. There would be no need to disturb the buildings on part of that site – a house, stables and a carpenter's shop – and the Council would benefit from a permanent building instead of having to rely on their present arrangement of renting a room and a stable and coach-house for their horse and cart. The Chairman recalled in his remarks that a Town Hall had been mooted as far back as the Jubilee of 1887 (there had also been an attempt to commemorate that occasion by some benefit for the hospital), but "one or two circumstances" had cropped up to prevent these schemes being brought to fruition.

Not for the first time, nor the last, were there rumblings of concern, even discontent, from the members of the public present: had the Council calculated the cost of such a scheme? Would there have to be an increase in the rates? Were high rates not already driving people out of the town? The response, equally predictable, took the form of an attack on the negativity of the comments: those present should have a little public spirit and not veto everything which would keep Petersfield in the background for ever; people should not be so niggardly and such stick-in-the-muds that they wanted to remain in the Petersfield of their grandfathers; Petersfield should be a progressive place. After a vote unanimously in favour of the Town Hall proposal, the matter was left with the UDC for consideration. To state that it remained contentious and therefore unresolved would be an understatement: it was not for another 33 years that a new Town Hall was finally built.

If the discussions regarding the building of a new Town Hall had been protracted and ultimately unresolved, those dealing with the celebrations for the impending Coronation passed off remarkably smoothly. However, it was announced in June 1902 that, due to Edward VII contracting a form of appendicitis which had required an operation, the Coronation would be postponed for two months. In Petersfield, it was decided to retain some of the celebrations on the original date. A shortened version of the whole Coronation Festivities was enacted on the new official day, with a general holiday for shops and businesses, thanksgiving services in the churches and a carnival and procession round the town in the afternoon, followed by sports, a tea and other amusements on the Heath, attended by an estimated crowd of 3,000 people from the whole district.

One 85-year old gentleman living in Sheep Street was interviewed in the press who could recall the events in Petersfield during Queen Victoria's Coronation – when he was 20 years old! The chief feature of the day's events had been a dinner for the inhabitants (Petersfield's population in the 1830s was around 1800). Tables were placed in the Square and down the High Street; the local innkeepers shared the catering and the beer was abundant; afterwards, "dancing was freely indulged in", with a band from Liss. This same gentleman had tolled the knell in St. Peter's Church on the death of King William IV in 1837; since William had reigned for just 7 years, the gentleman was also able to remember his predecessor, George IV.

The Boer War

Many townsfolk at this time were anxious about the fate of the Hampshire Volunteers fighting under Lord Kitchener in the Boer War, which had begun in October 1899. After fifteen months of fighting, the return of the Petersfield Company of the 3rd Volunteer Battalion Hants regiment under their commander Captain P.W. Seward, was therefore a cause for much celebration. Bunting decorated the High Street, Dragon Street, College Street and Lavant Street and, on emerging from the railway station, there was a huge triumphal arch erected by the Fire Brigade with a "Welcome Home" banner across it.

Captain Seward and his men were officially welcomed home by John Bonham-Carter (who had bidden them farewell at their departure), W.B. Edgeler (chairman of the Reception Committee) and the Vicar of St. Peter's; the contingent then marched through the town, accompanied by the Buriton Brass Band and various notables; finally, a service of thanksgiving was conducted in a packed St. Peter's Church. It was noted that the regiment had departed as soldiers of the Queen, but had returned as soldiers of the King. The following week, a public dinner for 250 guests was arranged at the Drill Hall for the homecoming "I" Company soldiers.

The Petersfield Musical Festival

The history of the Petersfield Musical Festival has been recounted in detail elsewhere, but it cannot be ignored here; it not only represented a fine new initiative by a small group of individuals who doggedly persevered with their ideas until they took firm hold within the community, but it also tapped into and awoke the latent talent of local musicians, young and old, whose collective efforts were to inspire generations to come.

The Festival was, essentially, a transplant from the Lake District town of Kendal, whose own Festival of Music was attended by Edith and Rosalind Craig-Sellar of Littlegreen (then a private house) in Compton, West Sussex, in 1897. Back in Petersfield, the sisters' efforts to reproduce such a festival were supported first by John

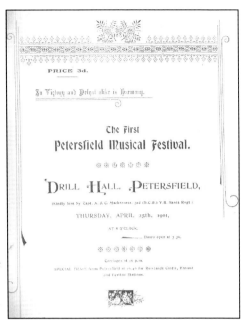

Notice for the first Petersfield Musical Festival

Bonham-Carter and A.J.C. Mackarness and then, as the enthusiasm for choral competitions among schoolchildren developed, so did a whole panoply of musical endeavour.

The inauguration of the Petersfield Musical Festival took place in the Drill Hall in April 1901, eliciting the comment: "In this praiseworthy venture, we hope to see the beginning of a real transformation in the character and quality of village choral singing in this locality". Six choirs, comprising 200 singers, took part in the event in the Drill Hall in

The choirs rehearse in the Drill Hall

Dragon Street, the venue for the Festival for the next 33 years. One third of the Hall was occupied by the tiered stage for the six choirs which took part. *The Hants and Sussex News* was highly enthusiastic about the new venture:

> *The first Petersfield Musical Festival has come and gone, and left in the minds of all who were associated with it either as competitors, performers or audience, the memory of a notable, delightful and thoroughly profitable day, which will not easily be effaced.*

The press devoted much space to a critique of the choirs competing, the competition for female voices, the madrigal and sight-reading competitions, and an appreciation of the 35-piece orchestra which gave an evening concert.

The event had been staged thanks to strong financial support from some fifty subscribers, and further substantial guarantees of money, if required, were made by four potential new donors.

This auspicious beginning was renewed during the years of the Edwardian era, with the second Festival eliciting the press comment: "Not many places the size of Petersfield, we venture to think, can rejoice in a gathering of this character, already so flourishing, and having the promise, we believe, of much greater prosperity and benefit yet to come". By 1903 and the third Festival, it had

Petersfield Choral Society, 1905

expanded to become a two-day event and marquees had to be hired for use as cloakrooms and refreshment tents; over 600 chairs also had to be hired – half of them from the Corn Exchange – and a new door was constructed halfway down the hall to provide an emergency exit. With 200 choir members and an orchestra of 50 on the wooden stage built each season, together with an audience of around 500 each year, greater safety and more ventilation were necessary.

The Festival continued to grow – both in numbers of participants and days of performance – until, by 1904, it had already reached three days in length, with a chorus of 100 children singing on the first day. The following year, the editor of *The Hants and Sussex News*, Frank Carpenter, assessed that "in time to come, the Festival will play an even more conspicuous part in the history of the town and neighbourhood". How right he was.

A measure of the interest, even excitement, produced by this annual event in Petersfield's calendar was the scene in the vicinity of the Drill Hall, when the town was enlivened by the influx of the choirs and a very large number of people who drove up or left in carriages or motor cars, or arrived by special trains from Portsmouth and Haslemere.

Petersfield School girls' choir, 1913

By 1908, both the Craig-Sellar sisters had married (Edith was now Mrs Stewart Gemmell and Rosalind, Mrs Alexander Maitland) and, although they had both left Petersfield, they returned to the Festival to present the prizes. The following year, the expansion of the event was such that *The Hants and Sussex News* devoted a supplement to the reviews of each of the competitions, with reports of the judges' remarks, and photos of the conductors appeared in the paper for the first time.

The churches

Attendance at Petersfield's church services at the turn of the century was impressive: around 350 parishoners attended the morning service at St. Peter's on Sundays and 550 in the evening. About 50 schoolchildren can be added to these figures and Steep had their own sizable congregation of about 60 people. The clergy gave regular instruction in the schools at this time. One complaint from all clergy was that there was an intolerable degree of drunkenness in the town and that public houses were open during the times of church services.

St. Peter's Church in 1913

The major event of 1902 was the building of the new Wesleyan Church in Station Road [now the Methodist Church], ten years after St. Laurence's Church had been

The Victorian interior of St. Peter's

established on the opposite side of the road. The new church was built to replace the former Wesleyan chapel in New Way [now St. Peter's Road], dating from 1871, which had become far too small for the ever-increasing Methodist congregation.

The new Wesleyan Church was built with a grant of £1,000 from the "20th Century Million Guinea Fund" and other grants and loans from a General Chapel building fund. The Methodists had increased their membership enormously in recent years and had far outgrown their chapel in St. Peter's Road [now St. Peter's Church Hall]. It was intended that Petersfield become the leader within the Surrey and North Hants Mission. The Rev. A.J. Summerhill, whose energy and enthusiasm had been largely responsible for the project, said, quite categorically, that "our site is central, conspicuous, convenient, one of the best sites in Petersfield, in fact, and our church is to be worthy of it: striking, substantial, beautiful, an acquisition and an adornment to the whole neighbourhood". He continued: "As a church, we stand for scriptural, evangelical, Protestant Christianity, but the aggressive, high Anglican, Romanising section we are pledged to withstand, everywhere and always."

The new Wesleyan Church, 1902

The building could hold a congregation of 300, with a schoolroom and smaller classrooms, a church parlour, and a covered way leading from the school to the church.

Plans for a new Primitive Methodist chapel in Station Road, on the corner with Windsor Road, were also approved in 1902 and the foundation stones were laid for a church and a Sunday School room on the site, which had been bought from Lord Hylton for £250. It was designed by T.E. Davidson of London, to seat 200 worshippers and built by John Holder of Sheet. Despite the fact that Primitive Methodists had only been established in Petersfield for three years, the new church enabled them to take over the Circuit (for a preaching rota) previously centred around Buriton. The Wesleyan and Primitive Methodist churches in Petersfield continued to operate in parallel well beyond 1932, the year of the Methodist Union.

The new Primitive Methodist Chapel, 1902

Although four new churches had been built in Petersfield in the space of twenty years, between 1883 and 1903, church ministries in the area had existed and itinerant preachers had practised for a good deal longer. The Congregational Church in College Street [now the United Reformed Church] for example, was a Free Church founded in the late eighteenth century by a Church of England clergyman, Mr. John Eyre, one of the founders of the Church Missionary Society; along with

Members of the Congregational Church, c.1900

Richard Densham, who became the first ordained minister of Petersfield's Congregational Church, they had set up a "village itineracy" to rural districts near London. At first, their preachers had been met with "awful persecution and strife" and been pelted with stones wherever they ventured. However, in Petersfield "they determined to stick and not be driven out". They were also responsible for starting the first Sunday School in Petersfield. Their chapel was demolished in 1883 and the present building erected in its place.

When, in 1902, the founder and superintendent of the Petersfield Band of Hope, Mr W. Joy, decided to take his retirement after 30 years in the post, he announced that the institution should be disbanded and the children in its care handed over to their respective denominations, allowing the Sunday Schools to take over his work. This non-sectarian organisation, aimed at training children in the principles of temperance, thus appeared to be passing into history, having played its part in the great Temperance Movement of the Victorian era. However, at St. Peter's Church, a new Band of Hope was started that December.

A branch of The Salvation Army had been instituted in Petersfield in 1886, in a "barracks" in Back Lane [now Swan Street], a building donated by John Gammon, the Petersfield builder and local councillor, who was a friend of the Salvation Army's founder, General William Booth. General Booth himself visited Petersfield in 1905 during one of his motor tours, and, on the Petersfield corps' 21st birthday celebrations two years later, the Guildford Salvation Army Band provided music in the town throughout the day.

One significant departure at the end of the Edwardian era was that of Canon F.J. Causton, who had been vicar of St. Peter's for 23 years. The number of parishioners who had contributed to his farewell testimonial amounted to between 600 and 700, a fine testimony to his standing and respect in the town. His family had also contributed to their legacy: his wife had been active in Sunday Schools, his daughters had started a Choral Society, and Canon Causton himself had served on the Petersfield School Board, as a Governor of Churcher's College, President of the local Temperance Council and the driving force behind the Workhouse Chapel. He finally left Petersfield upon his appointment as Master of St. Cross in Winchester. He was replaced by the Rev. Archdall M. Hill.

The Rev. Canon F.J. Causton

Education

The 1880 Education Act had brought in compulsory school attendance for all children up to the age of 10, but, for poorer families, ensuring their children attended school proved difficult as it was more tempting to send them out to work if the opportunity to earn an extra income was available. A further Elementary Education (School Attendance) Act in 1893 had raised the school leaving age to 11, and this was again raised, to 12, in 1899.

In Petersfield's Board Schools, situated between St. Peter's and Hylton Roads, there were 239 boys and 173 girls at the beginning of the Edwardian era. However, the Boards which had been set up in 1870 under the Forster Act, now found themselves abolished by the new Balfour's Act of 1902, which created Local Education Authorities for the first time, to organise funding, employ teachers and allocate school places. This meant that the duties and responsibilities of the old School Board passed to the Hampshire County Council.

Of statistical interest is the fact that there had been just 319 children (composed of 116 boys, 110 girls and 93 infants) in the three schools in 1892, the year when the British School in College Street was discontinued as a separate school; by 1898, the total had risen to 494 and, in 1902, 625 (which included the

Standard II, Petersfield Boys' School, 1912

children of Sheet, for whom the Board was now responsible.) Much more care was taken by the Board – and the courts – to ensure that every child attended school and there were severe penalties for parents who did not obey the law.

The Petersfield School Board was seen as a good example to the rest of the county in this respect and John Bonham-Carter and Mr W.C. Burley, as Chairman and Clerk respectively, won plaudits from the other members of the Board for their work over many years. In a report written by a Dr. Sadler for the County Council in 1904, it was stated that Petersfield should be made one of the chief centres for secondary education within the county. The premise for this was that *"Churcher's College well deserves further assistance as it may require to maintain a high level of intellectual efficiency in every branch of its work"*. Recommendations specifically for the College were for a new physics laboratory, additional classrooms, a Masters' Common Room and a reference library. The report continued:

> In considering the education needs of the district, of which Petersfield is the centre, I
> hesitated for some between two courses: (i) the provision of a higher elementary school
> for girls and (ii) the establishment of a well-staffed girls' secondary school. Finally,
> my judgement inclined towards the second alternative....and the best course would
> be to place it in Petersfield.

However, it was not until 1919 that this wish was realised and the County Secondary School for Girls was set up in the recently-vacated Dolphin Hotel at the end of the High Street [now Dolphin Court].

At Churcher's College, the Edwardian decade saw much progress in its educational provision. The Governors applied for Aid to the Local Education

Petersfield Girls' High School, 1919

Authority, so that they could offer classes in science, with specialised teachers and new laboratories. The new "science room" was completed in 1904, the same year as, with rising numbers of pupils, the school obtained a new gymnasium, sanatorium and cricket pitch, thanks to the generosity of its governors.

A memorial clock, dedicated to the memory of the late Mr W.B. Edgeler, a governor of the College for 12 years, as well as Chairman of the UDC, was placed in the tower above the north entrance to the College. A second memorial, in 1907, paid for by donations from pupils past and present and dedicated to the memory of John Bonham-Carter, the Chairman of Governors for many years, produced a new set of entrance gates for the school.

The Edgeler clock on Churcher's tower

Churcher's became an Aided Secondary School, which meant that they were expected to give maintenance allowances according to the means of the parents. The school was now full on the boarding side and its pupil numbers were rising slowly to the 100 mark. The formation of a Cadet Corps was considered and agreed. In 1905, on the occasion of the centenary of the Battle of Trafalgar, 55 boys (85% of those of eligible age) were admitted to the ranks immediately. The Corps was connected to the local 3rd Volunteer Brigade of the 6th Hants Regiment. Three years later, the Corps became part of the Officers Training Corps formed by the War Office with the aim of providing officers for the regular army, the special reserve and the territorial force.

Churcher's Cadet Corps, 1905

Bedales started life in Steep during the Edwardian period. In 1910, it was announced that two local teachers, A.E. Scothern of Bedales School and Douglas Welch of Churcher's College, had both signed amateurs' forms to play football for

Portsmouth in the 1911 season. Scothern, at 27, had already played a good deal of first-class football and had won amateur caps for England; he had played for Notts County the previous season. The 23 year old Welch had played for Cambridge University and Crewe Alexandra in the Birmingham League.

Bedales Main Block

The Scouting movement

The advent of Scouting in Petersfield occurred sporadically in 1908 and grew rapidly: three separate patrols had formed in the town that year under the supervision of a small group of local tradesmen (Messrs. W.H. Bradley, A. J. Mullet, and Reginald and Cecil Mould) and another troop had started at Bedales School. Their first weekend camps were held in June and July 1909 at Steep Farm and Uppark and their official recognition by the UDC came the same year.

Lieutenant-General (later Lord) Robert Baden-Powell's trial camp for 20 boys on Brownsea Island in 1907 and the publication of his *Scouting for Boys* the following year set the scene for, and created the ethos of, what was to become the largest youth organisation in the world.

Petersfield's own contribution to this history mirrored the enthusiasm and the energy which was developing elsewhere in the country: three separate patrols of boys were recruited by the end of 1908 under the supervision of Wilfred Bradley, a Lavant Street jeweller, Mr A.J. Mullet, a tailor and draper in Charles Street, and Reginald and Cecil Mould, sons of the builder, William Mould of Dragon Street.

After a public meeting at the Board School [now the Infants' School] in St. Peter's Road in the spring of 1909, the Petersfield Urban District Council voted to support the new venture by officially recognising their existence, and the 1st Petersfield Troop came into being. Mr E.R. Hillary, a draper in Chapel Street, became the official outfitter of the group and one

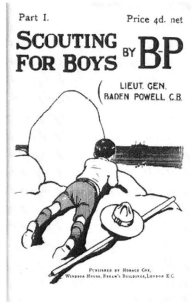

"Scouting for Boys", 1908

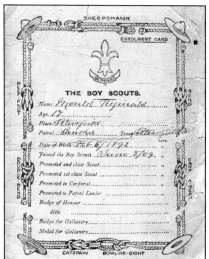

Reginald Mould's Scout's Enrolment Card, 1909

of his assistants, Alfred Herriott, was to be seen marching up and down outside the shop, not only causing quite a commotion in the town, but acting as the unpaid advertiser of the Troop. He was so successful that 50 boys attended the first camp at Uppark in August that year, when Colonel Featherstone-Haugh donated two fawns for their first (venison) supper! They also enjoyed their first campfire and practised some rifle shooting. Sadly, Herriott, described as "Petersfield's first Boy Scout...who initiated the movement" was also one of the first soldiers from the town to be killed in the First World War in 1914.

For their first headquarters, the Scouts used a room above the Square Brewery, rented to them but paid for by Mr. Bradley, where they undertook drill and physical exercises and started a programme of instruction which formed the major part of that first winter's activities. By 1910, the Troop was well established, with a management committee and executive committee in place, consisting mainly of Petersfield clergymen, high-ranking officers and professional people. At a meeting in 1910, a Captain Standish had been invited to speak about the formation of a Troop, based on his experiences elsewhere in the country. His plea to the newly formed Troop was that they should bear in mind that Scouting was a non-political, non-sectarian organisation and that they should all pull together to make it work in Petersfield. Mr Hillary's latest report showed that the Troop now numbered 40 boys and that Mr Bradley should be given all the support he needed to allow the group to continue and flourish.

The voluntary help offered and the generosity of the townspeople in general towards the new Movement (the population of the town at this time was around 4,000), ensured its success. Indeed, it was in 1911 that that Troop was reformed and renamed "The Petersfield Local Association of Boy Scouts", thus broadening its appeal to several neighbouring villages. It appointed a new Scoutmaster, the well-known High Street dentist, Mr C.F. (Charlie) Dickins, whose house and surgery were at Clare Cross [now part of Dolphin Court]. The Scouts had entered a new – and, as it transpired, a long-enduring – phase of its existence. Lord Selborne consented to be their first President and for the Troop to be called "The Earl of Selborne's Own".

Charlie Dickins

The Petersfield Troop soon numbered 60 boys. Some of them represented the town at King George V's Royal Review of 1911 and all of them attended Hampshire camps and rallies, giving gymnastics displays and, most importantly, creating their own entertainments to raise funds at the Corn Exchange [now Cubitt and West's]. A year later, the Movement was progressing rapidly, with Troops in Steep (Bedales School), East Meon, Langrish, Froxfield, Longmoor Camp, Bramshott, West Meon and Blackmoor, totalling 185 boys, including 5 King's Scouts.

By 1914, there was also a pack of Wolf Cubs in Petersfield for boys between the ages of 9 and 11, which met twice a week for instruction. It was in 1914, too, that the Troop began to operate a scheme which was to become their principal source of funding: the collection of old newspapers for sale as scrap paper for recycling. This was an activity which was to last for over seventy years.

"Defeat the Huns with Aeroplanes" – Wolf Cub project, 1914

The Corn Exchange "entertainments" (usually evenings of sketches, songs, recitations, pantomimes and comic operas), which began in 1913, were interesting inasmuch as they immediately preceded the operettas of Gilbert and Sullivan which began to be performed there in the 1920s. The Scouts were thus instrumental in bringing light opera to Petersfield audiences before the advent of the Operatic Society.

It was during the First World War that the Troop suffered from the absence of its leader, Charlie Dickins, at once the driving force and, frequently, the financial backer of all its activities. His replacement, Mr Hillary, kept the Troop active, while Mr. "Dickie" Weeks, subsequently a bandmaster at Churcher's College, continued to run the Bugle Band which had been formed in 1911. Like Charlie Dickins, Mr. Hillary gave freely of his own money to help the Scouts; he bought them a four-oared boat for them to practise for their Swimming and Boatman's badges on the Heath Pond.

Meanwhile, the Scouts helped in the war effort by providing assistance at a Soldiers' Canteen, knitting items for the forces or collecting donations for the war funds. But the most important innovation during these years was the move from renting the Square Brewery rooms to the purchase of a lease on the old Working Men's Institute in Heath Road for their meetings. It was probably the most decisive event in their history, since it not only represented a huge expansion and improvement in their activity space, but it gave them a coveted independence when they were eventually able to buy the building outright in 1920.

The Troop had the good fortune to be inspected by the Chief Scout and Lady Baden-Powell when they passed through Petersfield in April 1916. The District Commissioner. the Petersfield solicitor Mr A.J.C. Mackarness, had referred to the three King's Scouts in the Troop, indicating that they were proof of the success of the Troop as a whole, a view reiterated by Baden-Powell himself when he congratulated them on "the evident progress being made in spite of all difficulties incident to the war".

When, to everyone's relief, Charlie Dickins returned to Petersfield in June 1919 and resumed his brilliant leadership of the Troop, it was to be his lifetime's dedication; he worked indefatigably with the 1st Petersfield Scouts right up to his death in 1962 at the age of 80. It was a further stroke of luck for Petersfield's Scouts that another dedicated individual, Eric (Buster) Hampton, willingly took over the leadership and carried it through to his retirement in 1988. Two men, therefore, were, almost single-handedly, responsible for the maintenance of a Scout Troop in Petersfield for a total period of 80 years. There can be few Troops in the country that can better that record of service.

Fairs and Shows

The Taro Fair, 1906

According to the report in The Hants and Sussex News in October 1901, the annual Taro Fair, essentially seen at the time as a "cattle and pleasure fair", brought "a plentiful supply of horse and horned stock", but prices remained indifferent. By contrast, the afternoon and evening amusements were the largest recorded, stretching right across the Heath to within a few yards of the cricket ground and comprising "the usual variety of catchpenny attractions: shooting galleries, refreshment booths, coconut shies, knock'em-downs, swing boats and illuminated steam roundabouts."

In Edwardian times, "the sixth of October" was a red-letter day in the calendar of many people in the country districts around Petersfield, but, as is still often the case, poor weather depleted the number of visitors and this especially affected the "caravan folk" who usually arrived the day before the great event. The Taro Fair was characterised by deafening music,

The Taro Fair, 1912

whether from the beating drums and clashing cymbals at the stall, the cries of the stallholders themselves, or the organs on the roundabouts.

The chief purpose of the Fair was to provide a market for the sale of animals – livestock, horses, sheep and cattle – but it also provided a commercial opportunity to ventriloquists, distributors of tracts and gospel preachers. In Edwardian days, Biddall's and Chipperfield's shows with cinematograph pictures were most popular, as they offered the most up-to-date technological entertainment.

Around the fairground, people threw confetti and squirted water everywhere. To police all this legal mayhem required the import of a strong force of constabulary on duty, but the Fair was said to have been particularly successful when, the following day, "not a single case required the attention of the magistrates".

In 1906, Frank Carpenter, editor of *The Hants and Sussex News,* wrote:

> *The meaning of the name "Taroo" or "Taro" has often puzzled people ... but we think we are right in stating that it owes its origin to the Welsh drovers who in former times used to frequent the Fair, travelling by road with cattle from places as far distant as Barnstaple. There are some old inhabitants of Petersfield still living who can well remember the beasts being re-shod in meadows in the Causeway after their long journeys. The welsh for a bull is tarw, pronounced "taroo" and the use of this word by the drovers gave the Fair its popular title.*

Petersfield's second annual fair, "The Square Fair", was abolished in 1902 by order of the Home Department after representations from the UDC. This fair, which had taken place in July each year, was also owned by Lord Hylton and had been set up under the Fairs Act of 1871 to unite the previously held fairs commemorating St. Peter and St. Andrew. This was a disappointment, as it had enjoyed a revival in the later 1890s, with roundabouts, swing boats, coconut shies, shooting galleries and stalls in the Market Square.

The Horse Show, 1912

The number of annual shows and fairs in Petersfield at this time was considerable: the one constant in the calendar was the Taro Fair in October, but regular fixtures also included a Horticultural Show every August, a Horse Show in September, and an Autumn Show in November, thus illustrating the rural background and heritage of the town. The venues for these events varied, since the availability of open fields or private land close to the town centre was almost unlimited.

The Horse Show, 1912

The Horse Show had been inaugurated in 1891 and provided a wide programme of events: there were displays of cart horses, ponies and hunters, but also harness classes and jumping competitions. Local people were extremely knowledgeable about such matters and were keen to hear the judges' decisions. The event was held at different locations, often at Rookesbury Park in Wickham, the seat of the South Hants. M.P., Mr Arthur Lee, and sometimes in Petersfield at Aldersnapp Meadows, owned by Mr W. Nicholson and the home of Mr. James Chalcraft. At the 1905 Show, there were 1500 visitors to watch the 26 competitions – many coming by train from Portsmouth.

The Autumn Show, also founded in 1891, took place in the Corn Exchange, and consisted of an exhibition of farm and garden produce, such as corn and hay, fruit and flowers, butter and poultry. The various classes of entries provided local growers and producers with an up-to-date and comparative assessment of developing farming methods and an opportunity to receive prizes awarded for each category. Visitors came from a wide area around the town and enjoyed the colourful and picturesque show, while being entertained by a string band during the afternoon and evening. Any produce not claimed at the finish of the evening was sold by auction the next day.

Empire Day was a concept defined in the latter years of Queen Victoria's reign, which would "remind children that they formed part of the British Empire and that they might think with others across the sea what it meant to be sons and daughters of such a glorious Empire". The image it projected was that of Queen Victoria, the maternal head of an Empire covering almost a quarter of the globe and over 400 million souls. In fact, the first Empire Day was celebrated on 24th May, her birthday, but not until after her death, in 1902, and, although there was general public enthusiasm and support for an Empire Day, it was not recognised as an official annual event until 1916.

Each year after this, millions of schoolchildren and adults would gather to salute the Union flag and sing patriotic songs. Empire Day remained part of the calendar for more than 50 years but, after the gradual loss of Empire and the feeling that its jingoistic message was no longer politically correct, it became Commonwealth Day in 1966 and reverted to being held on 10th June, Queen Elizabeth II's birthday, in 1977.

In Edwardian times, Empire Day flourished throughout the United Kingdom and Petersfield was no exception to this: in 1907, for example, the Union Jack was hoisted on St. Peter's church tower and

Empire Day

many other buildings, and some of the townspeople wore a daisy, the flower most associated with the anniversary. A concert was held in a flag-and-bunting-bedecked Corn Exchange; the names of the British colonies were displayed on banners suspended around the room, and the evening progressed with music, speeches and the singing of patriotic songs such as Hearts of Oak, Jerusalem and God save the King.

With the benefit of hindsight, it is easy to see the irony – but also the prescience – in the content of one of the speeches that day: Mr Montague Kirkwood, of the East Hants Conservative Association who presided over the gathering, spoke of the size of the Empire, and the paramount importance of keeping open the means of communication between its different parts, including the seas. He referred to the huge navy which Germany was building and that "one could not but come to the conclusion that she was determined, it might be at no far distant date and whenever any opportunity offered, to become the aggressor. Against whom would the attack be directed if it was not the power which had the supremacy of the sea?"

The following year, 1908, the first formal local celebration of Empire Day took place, when Petersfield and Steep joined forces to commemorate the day under the Chairmanship of Dr. Cross. Schools were closed and shopkeepers also shut for the afternoon. The Steep schoolchildren marched to Petersfield, where they met their opposite numbers from the town and, together, they celebrated the occasion in the Square with a procession, music, marching by the Churcher's College Cadets, and a multitude of flags.

Crime and the Police

The police found themselves embroiled in some sensational local affairs in the Edwardian era: the two most heinous crimes which remained in the public folk memory for many years to come were the 1904 "Petersfield Beer House tragedy" and the 1906 "Mad Sailor affair".

In 1904, *The Spain Arms* pub stood at the corner of The Spain and Sheep Street [now no. 1 The Spain], where the landlord was a Mr Edwin Daughtry, who also worked as a cowman for the Seward family. He used to have up to 18 lodgers at the pub, often Italians, and always itinerant labourers. Over the weekend of the "tragedy" in July that year, there were seven Italians and a few English labourers, including a potato seller, a scissors grinder and his daughter.

The Spain Arms in 1897

After a bout of drinking, there had been an altercation between the two nationalities and one of the Englishmen, named Campbell, challenged one of the Italians to a fight in the garden. While the two men were setting about each other, the other Italians rushed at Campbell from behind and struck the Englishman, one – an organ grinder – with an organ stick, the other with a cobbler's iron last, kept at the inn for use by lodgers to repair their boots. Campbell, already the worse for wear from drink, had his skull fractured and he fell to the ground. The landlord sent him off to be cared for in the Workhouse, but he died there a few days later.

Meanwhile, the Italian workmen disappeared from Petersfield and it took three years before they were eventually tracked down in Luton. The case finally came to Winchester Assizes in November 1907, when the Italian organ grinder, Giuseppe Cuppo, was accused of "feloniously killing and slaying" James Campbell, a bricklayer. However, when charged with the offence, he claimed never to have been near the *Spain Arms*, and, although he was picked out by the landlord at an identity parade, others were not so certain that he was the right man. In his defence, Cuppo provided an alibi, stating that he was in Italy at the time of the incident and, with uncertainty as to his identity, coupled with the witnesses' cloudy memories after such a long time lapse since the event, the jury had to find him not guilty and he was discharged.

In the meantime, *The Spain Arms* had gained a new landlord. This was Alfred Shepherd, a long-time resident of Petersfield, a chimney sweep by trade, and a widower of 52 with four children who all lived with him in the inn. Tragically, he committed suicide there late in 1906 and the verdict on his death was that of "suicide whilst temporarily insane". Petersfield had seen several suicides in the town that year.

The presence of Italians in England was by no means uncommon: in the 1870s, the main regional origins of Italian emigrants to Britain had been from the Parma valley in the north, and the Liri valley, half way between Rome and Naples. The people from Parma were predominantly organ-grinders, while the Neapolitans made ice cream. Italians never settled in great numbers in the northern cities of Britain. By 1901, the Italian population was 4051 but their communities were becoming more affluent and, at the outset of the First World War, they were well-established in London; there were nearly 20,000 Italians in the United Kingdom in 1915.

One day in August 1906, a sailor from HMS *Nelson*, who had been at musketry practice earlier that day at Tipnor range and was still in uniform, came up the Portsmouth Road to Petersfield with a loaded rifle and bayonet attached. Half a mile outside the town, he began a shooting spree, first aiming a few shots at a cottage, then fired some rounds at a soldier on a bicycle. Next, he threatened a man on horseback, who immediately went to alert the police. Once the alarm had been raised, people came to witness the succeeding events: the man hurried quickly along Dragon Street, terrifying the townsfolk with his random shooting and hitting a cyclist in the knee. A police sergeant and two constables approached him, but withdrew when they, too, were threatened. The man proceeded along High Street, Chapel Street and eventually reached Station Road, threatening people all the while and firing indiscriminately at them.

It was close by the station that he shot a 36-year old mother, named Mrs Treble, in the thigh and she fell to the ground. She had been staying with friends in West Meon and was walking with her small daughter to the stables at the Railway Hotel, opposite the station. The man continued on his way, went over the railway crossing and was pursued for about a mile along the Winchester Road towards Stroud by police and others on bicycles. At this point, a man armed with

The Railway Hotel

a shotgun who had witnessed these events crossed the meadows near *The Seven Stars* pub and brought the sailor down. The police approached him, handcuffed him and took him back to Petersfield police station in a van.

A few days later in court, he gave his name as Joseph Burbidge, but it transpired that this was a false name and his real name was in fact Cyril Mitchell. Mrs Treble died of her wounds in the Cottage Hospital, but, although Mitchell was found guilty of murder, the local doctor present at his examination, Dr Cross, declared that he was suffering from "post epileptic mania" and he was pronounced "guilty but insane". He attempted to commit suicide while in custody, but was eventually committed to an asylum as a criminal lunatic.

Two other particularly shocking incidents occurred in 1907, when two young women were attacked near the town: one at Bell Hill, the other on Old Stoner Hill. Both attacks were accompanied by a demand for money with menaces, but, luckily, no serious harm was caused to the women concerned. The most unsatisfactory feature of the second assault was that no-one was brought to justice, as there had been insufficient evidence against any of the men who were brought to an identity parade.

The Workhouse was not without its share of problems for the police. In 1907, a "lively incident" involved an inmate, too drunk to be admitted to the casual ward, using obscene language and becoming obstreperous with the porter late one night. In such cases, the police were called immediately. The workhouse's population fluctuated constantly, usually depending on the season of the year. In February 1907, for example, there were the usual number of inmates – about 60 – but over one fortnight, 202 tramps had asked for relief, the majority having to be turned away without doing any work as there were only eight cells available for them.

Another "lively afternoon scene" one Sunday the same year concerned two drunken soldiers committing a savage assault on a policeman outside the Police Station in St. Peter's Road, having tried without success to enter *The Bell Inn* [now *Fusionbar*]. They were eventually overpowered, placed in the cells and, when they came to court shortly afterwards, were sentenced to 6 weeks' hard labour.

St. Peter's Road and the Bell Inn

National measures to combat drunkenness led to a new Licensing Bill in 1908, which had the desired effect of reducing the total number of licensed premises, as it was calculated according to the size of the population in a community. In the Petersfield UDC area, for example, there had been 16 fully licensed houses and 4 beerhouses recorded at the 1901

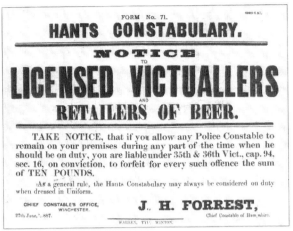

Police warning to pub owners, 1887

The Swan Inn (on left) in Chapel Street

1908 Licensing
Bill poster

The Swan Inn sign

The Golden Horse (on left)

The Dolphin Hotel [now Dolphin Court]

The Sun Inn [now JSW]

The Drayton Hotel, 1911 [now The Old Dairy]

census: this worked out as 1 for every 155 people in the town [the equivalent of having over 90 establishments today!]. Eleven of these were owned by Messrs G. Henty and Sons (*the Jolly Sailor, Crown, Fighting Cocks, Sun, White Hart, Blue Anchor, Drum, Swan, George, Golden Horse* and *Bricklayers' Arms*); four by W. and R. Luker (*the Dolphin, Red Lion, Railway Hotel and Market Inn*); two by Miss Amey (*the Bell and Royal Oak*);

and the remainder by other breweries. At a mass protest meeting in the Corn Exchange, there had been general, cross-party condemnation of the new Licensing Bill, originally brought in by Herbert Asquith when he was Chancellor of the Exchequer, before he became Prime Minster in 1908. Over the whole country, some 1300 to 1400 licensed public houses were disappearing every year. In Petersfield, it was also considered that there were some "superfluous public houses" and, in 1909, three of them lost their licences: the *Swan Inn* [at the corner of Swan Street, now the Prudential bank], *The Golden Horse* [named after the (erstwhile) gilded statue of William in the Square; now the site of Fat Face] and *The Spain Arms* [now a bed and breakfast establishment]. At the Corn Exchange meeting, it was stated that people could not be legislated into sobriety

The Royal Oak

and, although the incidence of drunkenness was being reduced, thanks in part to the Temperance Movement – strongly supported in Petersfield – it had nothing

to do with legislation. One speaker presented the view that public houses should be elevated to "places of light and decency like the continental cafés" instead of treating the "licence holder as an outcast and pariah". Plus ça change...

In 1910, there was a failed attempt by the UDC and RDC to purchase the old public house *The Fighting Cocks* [now the site of the Total garage in Dragon Street] for use as a common lodging house. It was thereby intended to relieve the workhouse of

STILL FALLING INTO LINE!
HOW IT DRUMS ON THE EAR.

DON'T forget the Drayton is not a "so-called" Temperance Hotel nor a Public Inn "so-called" Hotel. It is a Private Hotel where Wines, Spirits, and Beer (not guaranteed to be the best in the world) can be obtained from the Railway Hotel at a minute's notice if required. The Drayton has no need of the largest Bowling Green in the County. Visitors can not bend to play bowls after a good lunch.

Advert for the Drayton Hotel

its tramp population and offer a bed to any man who had enough ready money in his pocket to pay for it. The old pub went to a higher bidder, a Mr Compton, who sought permission – and was granted it – to turn the building into a common lodging house. Unfortunately, it soon gained a reputation for disruptive behaviour and many of the tramps were thrown back out onto the streets.

At the Petersfield Petty Sessions, there seemed to be no end to the charges laid against noisy customers and those using bad language in the town's pubs, cruelty to animals, disorderly sailors, incidents of larceny and nuisances by tramps. At the Union Workhouse in 1906, there were 62 inmates, and no fewer than 175 tramps ("casual paupers"), including 16 women and 4 children, had passed through the support system and been "relieved". The major problem for the managers of the workhouse was the cost of funerals for the poor.

Motoring offences during the Edwardian period brought much public indignation. However, the real problem lay in the fact that motor vehicles and horse-drawn traffic were, inevitably, sharing the roads. A case brought before Petersfield Magistrates in 1904, for example, concerned a man and his wife who had refused to stop a motor car when requested to do so by a person in charge of a restive horse. The car driver was fined £2 and 19 shillings costs. In Langrish the same year, a man was summoned before the court for being asleep while in charge of a horse and cart and there were complaints in Liss of "fast locomotives" travelling at 6 m.p.h. (the term "locomotive" generally meant a steam-driven lorry or waggon, according to the Locomotive Act of 1878, and was still occasionally used to mean a motor car).

Amey's steam waggon

In 1907, a well-known resident of Petersfield, Charles Money, wrote to the press complaining of the "motor terror". He quoted from a *News Chronicle* report he had read, describing a walk down a pretty country lane by a family who "were almost momentarily sickened by vile stenches befouling the air, from motor oils or gases, or smothered with filthy clouds of powdered refuse, raised by these rushing engines of impurity". Mr Money saw the vogue for motoring as an example of intolerable upper-class tyranny and wondered "how much longer are these abominable outrages on the rights and well-being of the people to continue?"

Victorian cycling

The Roads Committee of the Urban District Council had debated the issue of speeding cars in 1902, and recommended that the County Council be asked to make application to the Local Government Board for a ten miles per hour speed limit to be imposed through Petersfield. Some councillors felt that this was absurd and that such a bye-law would become a nuisance.

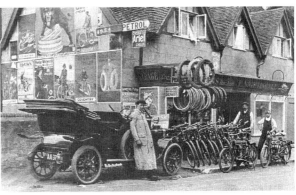

Edwardian motoring

Their arguments that "a decent horse could go more than ten miles an hour" and "bicycles came down from Butser cutting at more than 15 miles per hour" failed to persuade the majority on the Council to increase the speed, however, and the motion – to limit the speed of cars to 10 mph within the town – was carried. The Chairman concluded the discussion with the remark that: "a much more dangerous thing than motor traffic were the boys and girls who hired bicycles just as it was dark and ran round corners at 50 miles an hour".

In 1906, the question arose: "Should ladies drive motor cars?" Several correspondents to the *Hants & Sussex News* suggested that it was "not ladylike" and that "no woman has sufficient nerve" for the practice, but it was pointed out that, at the Glasgow to London run and the 1,000 mile trials in 1903 and 1904, a Miss Dorothy Levitt had driven high-powered De Dions and Napiers better than many male competitors. This ended the debate.

The new experience of motor cars began, for the first but certainly not the last time, to cause a nuisance to the general public, especially those who owned properties on main highways. They complained of the smell, dust and noise raised by the new vehicles – the latter explained, even if not acceptably so, by the fact that it was caused by the sucking action of the pneumatic tyres on the road surface. One such incident was reported by a Rural District councillor who stated that "two or three ladies going to a garden party in a landau met a motor car and were smothered in dust – they were not fit to be seen!" The onus was on car owners to find a remedy to this, as the cost of granite and/or tar to resurface the roads was too prohibitive.

It was declared that, ideally, cars should not be driven at more than 8 mph and, to this end, "motor traps" were instigated. The foot of Adhurst Hill, Sheet, was a place much favoured by police for catching drivers and, in 1909, three speeding offences were committed here and the perpetrators were committed to the Petty Sessions at Petersfield the following week. Although it was common for motorists to blow their horns when approaching a bend or an obstruction, it was also common for children – and in one case, a courting couple – to wander onto the roadway. Fines were levied and instructions given to motorists not to drive at more than 15 miles per hour.

A "sensational robbery" took place at Amey's Brewery at Christmas 1904, when an employee absconded with over £100 from the firm. Despite having used several aliases, he was later arrested in London and brought to Petersfield Police Station, where he was remanded in custody. At the Police Court the following month, he was charged with numerous counts of fraud and committed for trial at the next Assizes. He had had previous convictions and prison sentences and was sentenced to three years' imprisonment with penal servitude.

The Market question

The Market Square, 1908

Photographs of the market taken in Edwardian times show the whole area filled with livestock, and farmers and breeders involved in earnest discussions with auctioneers, potential buyers and sellers. Yet it was a turbulent time for all: those directly involved in market trading, local ratepayers and the Urban District Council were battling against the uncertainty of the market's very existence, its cost, its location and its possible loss to the community after eight centuries of establishment under the town's historic Charter.

Control of the heath and the market, the former the shared responsibility of Lord Hylton and Mr. John Bonham-Carter, the latter exclusively the right of Lord Hylton as Lord of the Manor, came under discussion early in the new century. This signalled the beginning of the end of the Hylton (and, hence, the Jolliffe) connection with the town. The family's withdrawal from the affairs of Petersfield took a decade to effect, but, with the sale of all their properties in 1911, the association had finally been severed. The Edwardian era was thus the swansong of the Jolliffe-Hylton family in the town and the age of social and political deference could be said to have been largely brought to a close.

It was in the summer of 1901 that the Urban District Council first heard of a communication between Lord Hylton's agent and the UDC Chairman to the effect that the Council were being offered control of both the Heath and the Market. The UDC were not anxious to gain control of the Heath, but were very much in favour of owning the market. The Charter of Ancient Market Rights, vested in Lord Hylton as Lord of the Manor, was subsequently offered to the Council at £1,000. Initially, their response was to reject the offer as the amount seemed prohibitive, but it was later accepted after a strong vote in favour at a public meeting in December 1901 and duly ratified by the UDC in 1902. The UDC thus finally had full legal control of the market from January 1st 1903.

However, all was not solved, for at that 1902 ratification meeting a further debate took place regarding the location of the market and there was a call for its removal from the Square. The whole question of the insanitary nature of the then current market led to a reminder that the Board of Agriculture had not recommended its removal, but simply requested that the surface of the Square be renewed, so that it could be regularly cleansed. In 1903, the Market Committee of the UDC reported that "it might be advisable to purchase a [new] site and lay out a permanent market rather than expend a large sum on improving the Square".

The pros and cons of removing the market, spending vast sums on a new, first-class, sanitary marketplace (nearer the station, for example), or, alternatively, paving the Square, building better drainage and improving the checking of stock arriving and leaving the present market, became a *cause célèbre*. With uncertainty about the Board of Agriculture's real intentions, the possibility that they might eventually decide to close the market anyway, the fluctuations in the decisions made about the market by the ratepayers, all caused the debate to rumble on for several years.

The death, in April 1903, of Mr W.B. Edgeler, honoured in the press as "the leading spirit in all public affairs in Petersfield", occasioned an even sharper debate over the future of the market and not a little animosity between councillors. The man who replaced him on the Council was Mr J.P. Blair, not voted in so much for his personal qualities, but for his stance on the future of the market. Sensing that there was some support within the Council for removing the market from the Square, and accurately predicting the public's strong preference for retaining the market where it had been for centuries, he called a public open meeting in the Square which attracted a large crowd. His strenuous stance – the retention of the market – brought him widespread support. Despite a certain amount of scaremongering by Blair, who suggested that a new market site could cost the taxpayers £8,000, and calling it preposterous that anyone should complain about the eight hours a

The Market Square, 1914

fortnight that the market took up in the centre of town, his entertaining oratory easily won the day.

Meetings occurred thick and fast throughout 1903 and 1904, sometimes called at short notice via handbills or with the aid of the Town Crier. The fear that any approach to the Board of Agriculture would possibly result in the market being removed, in the long term if not in the short, was allayed by an inspector who assured those present at a meeting in June that the market was not destined to be removed from the Square – a remark greeted by loud applause.

In September, the UDC reported on what it called "the most important matter the Council has had to deal with since its existence". The Board of Agriculture's regulations for weekly markets were destined to be tightened in 1904 and the UDC believed it incumbent upon itself to bring in the new rules for Petersfield's fortnightly market in case the Board changed the regulations again at a later date. The new rules demanded the paving of markets with hard material and for the area to be swept and washed down thoroughly after each session.

Meanwhile, the council had weighed up the comparative costs of relocating the market to a new, improved site against spending a large amount of taxpayers' money on bringing the Square up to the necessary standards. Its Market Committee reached the conclusion that it was the right thing, from a financial point of view, to remove the market from the Square. "However", the Chairman added, "if the majority of the Council and the ratepayers are prepared, on a question of sentiment, to pay the additional annual amount for keeping the market in the Square, well and good".

Two months, two meetings and several hours of acrimonious discussion later, the UDC voted to concrete the Square (by 6 votes to 1, with 1 abstention) for the estimated maximum of £1000 that it would cost. Unfortunately, the Local Government Board refused to sanction a loan for the improvement to the Square and the matter of finding an alternative site was thrown back into the melting pot.

While it was evident that Lord Hylton had spent considerable sums on the market and was never questioned about it, by opening the decision-making democratically to the ratepayers, as some councillors suggested, there might be conflicting opinions expressed and therefore difficulty in coming to a conclusion on the matter. There was also the fear among councillors that the Board of Agriculture could close the market (for sanitary reasons) at a moment's notice, as had happened about ten years previously (this had been averted by Lord Hylton who had intervened personally by speaking to the Board's President!)

Yet another imponderable was Petersfield's need for new water and lighting provision, which was also going to cost the ratepayers money. This additional complication suggested that the question of a new market should be delayed for a couple of years. Those who favoured keeping the market at all costs admitted it was through sheer sentiment – the market was a picturesque relic of mediaeval times. Thus the sentimental arguments battled it out with the utilitarian. The debate ended with the resolution that the Council should investigate the cost of a new market elsewhere in town.

By May 1905, the contentious debate was still rumbling on without any definite conclusions being drawn. At a ratepayers' meeting, when 250 people were present, a large majority were in favour of retaining the market in the Square. At that meeting, a letter from Lord Hylton was read out, in which he refuted the suggestion that the Board of Agriculture was likely to remove the market – providing it was kept in a sanitary condition – and that he personally could not vote for its removal while it was flourishing.

A second public meeting the following month convened by some members of the UDC caused some controversy and noisy and "animated proceedings" among those present, the majority of whom appeared to approve the retention of the market in the Square. A letter from Lord Hylton was read

Petersfield Market.

NOTICE OF RESULT OF POLL OF OWNERS AND RATEPAYERS.

WHEREAS at a meeting of Owners and Ratepayers duly convened held on the 23rd day of May, 1905, the following resolution was proposed :—

" That having in view the opinion of the Board of Agriculture as to the unsuitability of the Square for the purpose of a Market, and also the refusal of the Local Government Board to sanction a loan to defray the expenses of repairing the surface of the Square, it is desirable to establish a market at some other suitable place in the Parish of Petersfield, and that the Owners and Ratepayers of the Urban District consent to the Urban District Council purchasing land and providing a market and all necessary works for the same."

AND WHEREAS the said resolution was not carried, but a poll was demanded, which has been duly taken.

I HEREBY CERTIFY that the result of the said Poll of Owners and Ratepayers is as follows:

Number of Votes for the resolution ... 420
Number of votes against the resolution 387

Dated this 26th day of June, 1905,

R. G. CROSS,
Chairman of the Petersfield U D.C.

Notice of the Vote to remove the Market, 1905

out which stated his view that "I think that every ratepayer will be a sufferer if it is moved". "Removers" and "retainers" had their opportunity to vote at a poll held a week later – at which the removers outnumbered the retainers by 420 votes to 387.

Yet another meeting of the UDC, characterised by "boisterous scenes" and "stormy discussions", took place three months later, at which irregularities in the distribution and collection of voting papers were queried and a call made for the poll results to be quashed. However, since there could be no new market within two years, the present (Square) site had to be improved and Lord Hylton consented to the concreting and repaving of the Square itself and to a kerb being installed. This work was carried out in 1906, along with the laying of tarmac on the roads on the east and west sides of the Square, at a total cost of £510.

The market question was still not resolved by the new elections to the UDC in 1906, when a majority of "removers" were returned. However, a Board of Agriculture inspector examined the Square early in 1906 and pronounced himself satisfied with the work that had been carried out, apart from a few defects in the paving which could be remedied. The market had thus had a temporary reprieve.

The Heath

During the Edwardian period, Lord Hylton was still considered as the Lord of the Manor. He had owner's rights to one third of the Heath Pond, the Heath itself and the annual Heath Fair. However, these rights were starting to be questioned – even eroded – and the decade was to see the emergence of a fairer and more democratic management of the urban and rural spaces within the Borough of Petersfield. As with the market rights, the democratically-elected Council began to assert its independence from any adherence to the ancient manorial rights which had served the community since the twelfth century. It goes without saying that such manoeuvres required tact and a delicate approach to their erstwhile masters. The inevitable question arose on both issues: whether the Square or the Heath might incur losses if they were run by the Council.

In 1901, a deputation from the Petersfield Working Men's Association was received by the UDC on the question of the Council taking over the Heath as a public recreation ground for the benefit of the inhabitants of the town and district. The Golf Club had already built their pavilion in the 1890s and were contributing five guineas a year towards the upkeep of the Heath.

As tenants in common of the two sections within Petersfield parish (the other third belonging to Buriton parish), Lord Hylton and Mr John Bonham Carter (Lord of the Manor of Buriton) had made an offer to the town later that year and it was

Lord Hylton himself who had proposed that the town take responsibility for the Heath. Councillor Thomas Woods, a housebuilder and always an outspoken, even contentious, member of the UDC, declared that Petersfield was fortunate in having the golden opportunity to acquire for a song what in other places – he cited Havant recreation ground as an example – cost hundreds of pounds to purchase. A debate ensued over the pros and cons of leasing versus purchasing, but Mr Woods' motion – to attempt to purchase rather than lease the Heath – was ultimately carried.

The sums asked for transferring the rental of the Heath and the Pond were £8 for Lord Hylton and £4 for Mr Bonham Carter, exclusive of the Fair, for which Mr William Mould was paying £8. The total rental price was therefore to be £20. Unfortunately, there were complications with the restrictive clauses relating to the use of certain parts of the Heath by the Golf and Cricket Clubs. The cricket club had laid its pitch on the Heath in 1856 and built its pavilion in 1880.

The Heath and Pond in the Edwardian era

By August 1902, the terms of the agreement between the UDC and the Lords of the Manors of Petersfield and Mapledurham (the historic name for the Parish of Buriton) for the purchase of the Heath were publicly known: the rights, including the Pond and the Heath Fair rights (previously under the ownership of Mr Bonham-Carter), were to cost £920. The Lords retained their jurisdiction over the felling of trees and the erection of buildings, the right of free fishing and boating on the Pond, and the use of the boathouse; by contrast, the cricket and golf clubs were to be granted free and undisturbed access to their grounds.

Sensing their future impotence with these unacceptable restrictions, the UDC took issue with the clauses dealing with the felling of trees and the construction of buildings, and this held up the negotiations for a further period of time.

The question of the management of the Heath appeared on the UDC's agenda again in 1904, when Councillor J.P. Blair complained of the "objectionable and dangerous beasts" (cattle!) which roamed there. During a recent visit by the Cooperative Society of Portsmouth, numbering 650 people, he said he had counted 46 head of cattle. He called for measures "to remedy this filth and nuisance", which made it almost impossible to take a pleasant walk on the Heath. In former times, an old man was employed to look after the Heath, but now there was no-one in charge. He called upon the Council to re-open negotiations with the Lords of the Manor for the purchase of the Heath "because the place was thoroughly mismanaged at the present time". Councillor Woods, seconding Mr Blair, added that, if the Council were to take on the management of the Heath, it could also

The Heath in Edwardian times

control the moral behaviour of the people who used it – citing the objectionable language and behaviour of certain "lads" as his main argument.

As was the case with the Town Hall and Market Square, however, the resolution of these thorny issues was left in abeyance. Indeed, the case for the leasing of the Heath had not been made; a team of Southampton solicitors declared on the subject of manorial rights as late as 1908 that "the Heath was not a public park or pleasure ground provided by the local authority. It was the private property of Lord Hylton and Mr Bonham-Carter". The Heath Pond, meanwhile, was the subject of even more controversy: people mistakenly thought that the Pond was dealt with under the latest Enclosure Acts (i.e. removed from the power of a Lord of the Manor in order to satisfy a growing demand for open

The Heath Pond, 1908

spaces for the health and exercise of the population at large). The UDC Chairman expressed his view that the Pond was, like other ponds, defined as free to all to fish, skate and boat on, which as they had had the right to do from time immemorial.

In 1910, the UDC made a further approach to the landowners, who were now willing to sell, and the Council subsequently applied to the Local Government Board for a loan of £1,100 to purchase the Heath. It took a public enquiry in May 1913 to resolve the problem finally, and the matter was officially concluded in January 1914, with £642 being paid to Lord Hylton and £400 to Lothian Bonham-Carter for this important piece of rural Petersfield.

The Heath saw its fair share of drama: the death of three young boys by drowning in the harsh winter of 1902 proved that any movement onto the ice by the public was dangerous. Two of the boys' school friends, together with the Hon. S.H. Jolliffe who lived at nearby Heath House and the Rector of Buriton had run to save them, but the boys had already been half an hour under the icy water before their bodies were recovered.

A happier event on the Heath later that year was the Sports Day organised to celebrate the Coronation of King Edward VII, with flat races, slow bicycle, egg and spoon, wheelbarrow, obstacle, tipping the bucket, skipping, and 1 mile walking races. The Working Men's Association held an annual fête on the Heath which consisted of cricket matches (between gentlemen and ladies in fancy dress), bowls and children's sports, all accompanied by a brass band and ending with an evening open-air concert and dance.

One contemporary aspect of the Heath frequently forgotten about is its use as a site for military manoeuvres. Local and other regiments used it as a training ground for infantry, but it was in 1903 that the whole of the Petersfield area, and especially that area centred around the Heath, became of utmost importance to Lieut.-General Sir John French and his 1st and 2nd Army Corps. Lieut-General French (later Field Marshal, the Earl of Ypres) had distinguished himself commanding the Cavalry Division during the Second Boer War and later became C-in-C of the British Expeditionary Force for the first two years of WW1.

Sir John French

In the early autumn of 1903, the Hants and Sussex News reported:

> From a quiet country town, pursuing the even tenor of its way, with only an occasional ripple of any great popular excitement, Petersfield was transformed for a couple of days into a conspicuous military centre teeming with troops of all descriptions, full of life and movement, and presenting scenes of the utmost variety and interest.

The manoeuvres were taking place over a wide area of Hampshire, Berkshire, Wiltshire and Oxfordshire, and were to be the most important and practical ever held in England. Upwards of 40,000 soldiers were involved in the exercise, whose aim was to re-create the imaginary scenario of an external force invading England from across the Channel. General French's task was to check the advance of this force. Militarily, the exercise was to represent a test between the old school of military strategists and tacticians, and the new.

A detachment of engineers had been busy over several weeks in making preparations for the encampment of a large body of men (approximately 15,000) in the vicinity of the Heath, supported by the Army Service Corps who had established a depot of stores for the exercise. Despite a day's postponement due to a hurricane on the expected day of the start of the manoeuvres, which had blown tents into the air, lifted tarpaulins from waggons and caused the horses to stampede, the manoeuvres were carried out successfully and General French declared himself so enamoured of the site that he spoke of the likelihood of bringing his troops to Petersfield again. The exercise had occupied two square miles of the Heath: the sandy soil lent itself to the tented encampment, drinking water for the men was obtained from the town mains and the horses were watered at the Pond. A large canvas tank was also set up near the sandpit on the Heath [by Music Hill] for the men to wash in.

Heath Farm, 1901

For the inhabitants of the town, the presence of such a massive force provided diversions in abundance. Sir John French himself was billeted at Allan Munday's farm [now Heath Farm]; many of the officers were billeted at the Dolphin Hotel and in private houses; the heaviest part of the military transport was parked in the Market Square for two nights, where there were thirteen traction engines and lines of trucks containing hundreds of tons of provisions and forage. The officers slept on the tops of loads of hay under canvas covers, with some of them finding space in the Corn Exchange. The townsfolk witnessed the long lines of motor cars and motorcycles of the Motor Volunteer Corps, military horsemen, transport waggons, and officers and men on foot coming and going throughout the two days. As the press noted:

> "picquets patrolled up and down and military police were everywhere in evidence, so that it required no effort of the imagination to picture Petersfield for the nonce quite in the possession of Tommy Atkins".

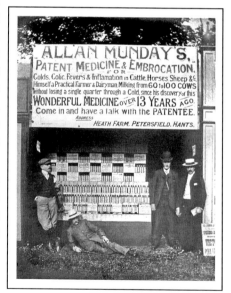

Allan Munday's patent medicine for animals

Commercial life

The Edwardian era seemed consciously to usher in a new optimism: rising prosperity brought the possibility of holidays for ordinary people; better health became a reality; and commerce reflected the awakening needs of communities by launching a new world of advertising and bold initiatives.

Petersfield was not immune from such changes. In the first decade of the 20th century, its population rose from 3,265 to 3,947, a relatively large surge when compared with the increases during the latter decades of the nineteenth century. Since the previous census in 1891, the population had doubled, although the size of the parish of Petersfield had been extended to include parts of the parishes of Sheet, Nursted and Weston. Sheet's population, for example, was 784 in 1891, but 228 of these people had been added to those of Petersfield by 1901. Other villages' populations were: Buriton (798), Steep (789 – including 96 at Bedales School), and Liss (1701).

A guide to the town was produced in 1901: the "Handbook and Guide to Petersfield", written by H.T. Webster Worrall, was published by S.J. Cole of Lavant Street. The first illustrated commercial advertisements appeared in the *Hants & Sussex News* in 1906, with a line drawing of Fuller's, the Lavant Street grocer's, incorporated into its usual publicity. It had been Mr W.J. Fuller who had led the campaign

SUSSEX NEWS—WEDNESDAY DECEMBER 17, 1913.

TELEPHONE No. 35.

GOODS FOR THE FESTIVE SEASON.

For Value!   For Quality!   For Variety!

W. J. FULLER

Respectfully invites an inspection of his stock and a perusal of his ......

XMAS PRICE LIST.

Cooking and Dessert Fruits from the CHOICEST IMPORTS OF THE SEASON. Biscuits in Fancy Tins, Chocolates, Fondants, English and French Confectionery.

Elves and Carlsbad Plums, Dates, Figs, Mincemeat, Plum Puddings.

XMAS CRACKERS Tom Smith's and other makers from 5½d. to 4s. per box. HUNDREDS OF BOXES TO CHOOSE FROM.

ORNAMENTED, ICED AND OTHER CAKES

From 1s. upwards.

Meringues, Swiss and Russian Pastry.

WEDDING & BIRTHDAY CAKES made on the Premises from the Purest Ingredients.

MINCE PIES.

Mild Breakfast Bacon, English and Irish Hams, Gruyere, Stilton, Caerphilly, Cheddar, Roakfort, Koboka and other Cheese, Cream: Sausages, Pork Pies, Ox Tongues, Soups, Potted Meats, &c., in Tins and Glasses.

TEA in Handsome Boxes suitable for Presents, 1s. and 2s. each.

HIGHEST QUALITIES AT LOWEST PRICES IN ALL DEPARTMENTS.

Orders collected and delivered Free in the town and district daily; Orders by Post receive PERSONAL ATTENTION. Any Article not in stock procured as quickly as possible.

W. J. FULLER, Tea & Provision Merchant, Bread & Cake Baker,

LONDON HOUSE, PETERSFIELD.

Raisins Stoned on the Premises by Patent Machinery.

for Half-Day closing in 1901 – rapidly agreed by other shopkeepers: a Thursday closure – from 2 p.m. – became the norm and was to last for the next 80 years. The local paper also began to carry adverts for the products of the Portsmouth firm of

FENDERS & FIRE BRASSES

we show every kind. You will find just the one addition you want to your home in our stock—something to brighten the room up.

OUR SHINING BRASS FIRE SUITES

make shining, bright, comfortable hearths, cheerful fireplaces against which it is a pleasure to sit. They make tasteful, elegant and substantial wedding presents too and they are not prohibitive in price.

A SPECIAL SHOW OF COAL VASES

is also a feature of our stock, and we have a beautiful variety in Wood, Brass, Copper and Japanned Boxes from 2s. 6d. to 25s., all fitted with linings and scoops.

LANDPORT DRAPERY BAZAAR,

Commercial Rd. & Arundel St.,

PORTSMOUTH.

Landport and even nationally known firms such as Bird's Custard, Cadbury's cocoa, Horlick's Malted Milk and Elliman's Embrocation.

ELLIMAN'S EMBROCATION

Neighbour's bakery and grocery in the Square

Llewellyn Bradley's Lavant Street Post Office

Cordery's of College Street

The town's growing prosperity was reflected in the elegant department store of Thomas Privett in the Square and the four high-quality grocery firms of J. P. Cordery ("the oldest and most reliable grocery establishment in Petersfield") in College Street, W.T. Neighbour's in the Square, Fuller's in Lavant Street and the International Stores in Chapel Street. In 1908 alone, Shepherd's Saddlery moved from the west side of the Square to larger premises on the east side [now occupied by Laura Ashley]; Whittington's "Gentlemen's Outfitters" extended their property at 1 Chapel Street [now a card shop]; and Mr Llewellyn Bradley's corner shop on Lavant Street [now Sue Ryder's] was altered to avoid it encroaching onto the pavement. Rowland & Son extended their premises in the Square in 1910.

There were several dairies in town, indicating the importance of the industry to Petersfield: Aylwin's in Hylton Road, Hunter's in the High Street, Norman's at Herne Farm, Smart's in The Causeway, Corbett's also in the High Street and Heward's Lythe Farm at Steep.

Certain physical aspects of the town also changed in 1901: some shops were added to the private houses in Lavant Street and extended their fronts to within 5 feet of the pavement – the beginnings of the random development which, sadly, is our legacy today. The west side of Chapel Street was completely re-built in the Edwardian decade and new large-scale housing developments had arrived in the shape of terraces in Station Road, Windsor Road, North Road, Tilmore Road and Penns Road (collectively known as the Heath Estate).

It was known that there was a great demand for houses by well-to-do people and the number of villas built at around this time attest to this phenomenon. One such example of this was the building of large properties along the road overlooking the Heath Pond, known then as Exercise Road [now Heath Road West].

Exercise Road

The arrival of the motor car produced the first garages in town: Britnell and Crawter's were established in College Street in 1907 and their garage [now the Folly Market] advertised itself as "Cycle and Motor Agents and Makers". As the motor car gradually displaced the horse and trap as a common means of locomotion, so the erstwhile trades associated with the latter became redundant. The most prominent of the town's blacksmiths was Mr D.E. Hobbs; he had begun business in the town in 1876 and held a number of civic positions in the late Victorian and Edwardian periods, including service

D.E. Hobbs, blacksmith

Britnell and Crawter's garage

as a UDC councillor for fifteen years and being its Chairman for three of these. He was finally rewarded for his public service to the community by being appointed a J.P. for Hampshire. He operated his forge in the small building at the back of Chapel Street [now Greggs' bakery] and, as the shoesmith's trade diminished, became a general "jobbing smith". He passed on his business to his son and, as Hobbs and Son, they traded in the construction and repair of carts and vans from new

The entrance to Hobbs' smithy

premises in Station Road and Swan Street, providing "every description of carts, vans, waggons, lorries, built to order on the premises". They were an excellent example of a family business adapting to the times.

In 1901, the new Petersfield and District Steam Laundry Co., situated in "the Rushes" [now Frenchman's Road] attracted special praise in the local press as an example of a prosperous industry, representing "many possibilities of good for the neighbourhood". In an article explaining the intricacies of the various processes at work, it clearly demonstrated that the laundry had "everything that science can suggest for the improvement and perfection of cleaning". Here was the latest technology at work – not merely for the town, but for the whole district, as goods were delivered from as far afield as Godalming, Witley and Haslemere. The firm employed between 30 and 40 people, its water supply came from its own well, but, to satisfy the sceptics of "progress", it prohibited the use of chemical bleaching and washing powders and used only "the best yellow soap".

The Petersfield and District Steam Laundry, 1901

The Steam Laundry main room

The 1905 extension

Two years later, the company turned in a profit of £500 for the year and tenders were invited for the enlargement of the buildings; in 1905, the laundry was extended to become the building which we still see today.

To help with collecting statistics for the impending census in 1901, the Building Committee of the UDC deemed it necessary to create a proper numbering system for houses in the town, to replace Lord Hylton's own numbers for his properties (still visible under the canopies of houses in Sheep Street). Ten years previously, there had not been any clear street nameplates, but this had also now been remedied.

Sheep Street – the Hylton numbering system

Commerce had suffered disproportionately in the first decade of the twentieth century through several outbreaks of fire in the centre of town. Although the Fire Brigade had only been called out once, in 1901, to a "fire of a trifling nature", an "alarming and disastrous fire" at Gammon & Sons' workshops in February 1904 was the worst seen for many years in Petersfield. At just past midnight, the steam saw mills, located at the junction of Station Road and College Street |now the site of Black Horse cottage| belonging to the old established firm of builders and contractors, were almost completely destroyed by a fire, luckily without loss of life. Mr T. Gammon himself and another man raised the alarm by running to the fire bell in the High Street and, without waiting for horses to arrive to pull the hose cart and fire engine, dragged them themselves to the scene.

Barely four months later, the Petersfield Fire Brigade engine house in St. Peter's Road |now public toilets| was extended and covered with a corrugated iron roof. Fifty percent of the cost for this was borne by local auctioneer Mr W.P. Jacobs, the Fire Captain, in preparation for a new steam fire engine to be delivered in July. This was the long-awaited Shand, Mason & Co. "steamer" which came into service immediately, together with a new fire alarm system for the town: an automatic alarm (triggered by breaking the glass casing) fixed outside the fire station and connecting to all the firemen's residences.

The steamer's first call-out came three months later, to a fire in Langrish, when its advantages were clearly demonstrated: it had more copious jets, it did not require manual pumping, and it was immediately ready to start work at the scene of the fire.

After nearly 18 years' service as Petersfield's Fire Captain, W.P. Jacobs resigned in 1906, to be replaced by Mr W.J. Tew.

Late on Christmas Eve, 1907, another serious fire partially destroyed Thomas Privett's outfitter's [now New Look] in the Square and, although there was no personal injury, it caused nearly £4,000 worth of damage, the almost total destruction of the main shop and the Christmas stock inside.

The fire bell (located on the roof of Rowswells) had summoned the hose cart, which was fetched by some of the remaining firemen who were not on holiday. Fortunately, the new Fire Captain, Mr Tew, had the assistance of several policemen and servicemen who were in the vicinity. On this occasion, the steamer was not needed, as water was pumped directly from two nearby hydrants in the Square.

W.P. Jacobs

As with the previous serious fire in 1904, its cause was never discovered. In a curious echo of this event, the same premises, later owned by another outfitter, Norman Burton, suffered the same fate in 1947.

A demonstration of the new "Minimax" fire extinguisher – the original model was invented and produced in Germany in 1903 – was held in the Market Square in 1908, when officers from the Fire Brigade used their hand-held machines to douse an artificially-constructed bonfire of wooden boxes soaked in paraffin and smeared with tar. As if to prove the machine's efficacy, a boy using one of the machines easily put out the resulting blaze.

The hose cart

Celebrating the 21st anniversary of the Petersfield Fire Brigade in 1910, Mr W.J. Tew recalled its history: during the first few years of its existence, the Brigade had been handicapped for want of appliances and it was difficult to find funding to support the service, several of their members having had to canvass for contributions from the public. After 1894, when Mr Jacobs took command, they were able to buy more apparatus after an appeal for funding from the public and the UDC. Over the previous 21 years, the total number of calls to the Fire Brigade had reached nearly 70 and the strength of the Brigade was 15 officers.

The Fire Brigade on parade, c. 1910

Cultural, leisure and sporting pursuits

Culturally, Petersfield's Literary and Debating Society and its home-produced Musical Festival attracted audiences from a wide region and, together with the multitude of entertainments at the Corn Exchange, provided the town's residents with a fine choice of cultural and leisure activities. Besides the numerous concerts and theatrical presentations at the Corn Exchange, there were popular evenings such as the "Penny Pops", with tableaux vivants, brass bands, instrumental music, sword swinging, recitations and singing. At such evenings, which usually took place in the winter months, there could be attendances of up to 600 people (i.e. nearly 20% of the population), as many as 132 performers, and a good spread of talent from the whole community. Front seats cost sixpence.

If funds needed to be raised, then a *café chantant* was often a popular choice for entertainment. These would last about three hours and consist of short theatrical performances, songs and music solos.

The Literary and Debating Society, with just over 100 members, provided a forum for general public debate, but, in the Edwardian era, it also convened the series of Oxford University Extension lectures on the subject of the French Revolution in 1912. The Society, which met at St. Peter's Hall, was the nearest the town had to an intellectual centre, with its open, public debates on matters of both local and national importance and its concern to bring to Petersfield quality speakers of national renown who would provide their members with an opportunity to tackle serious issues in an enlightened and comprehensive manner. It was not surprising, therefore, that in 1910 it was one of their group who proposed to amalgamate the existing five libraries around the town into one – potentially a future free library service for all residents. The committee looked to the UDC to offer such a service.

The Victoria Brass Band was formed by Fred Kimber and Mr Gale in 1901, although its survival became precarious over the years; there was even a hope that a bandstand could be built for them on the Heath, but this was never realised.

In the four years since its foundation, the Women's Institute's most successful enterprise was the annual Arts and Industries Exhibition held in St. Peter's Hall in 1904. About 250 exhibits were classed in thirteen

The Women's Institute [on right]

different sections for competition; these included needlework, woodcarving, pictures, photographs and cookery. By 1909, the Institute had expanded its annual event to 700 exhibits and, that year, it was held over two days in the Corn Exchange. In a short account of the brief history of the Institute, Mrs Loftus Jones*, a vice-president, outlined the aims of the Institute as a place of rest, recreation and instruction. Activities by and for members included lectures on First Aid and Home Nursing, classes on woodcarving, musical and social evenings and the formation of a branch of the Home Reading Union. Most recently, a lending library had been opened and was proving very popular. For the summer months, there was now a Tennis Club, organised excursions into the country and a garden party. Membership stood at 150.

[*Mrs Gertrude Loftus Jones was the wife of Admiral Loftus Francis Jones, who lived at Hylton House in The Spain, and the mother of Commander Loftus William Jones, Petersfield's only VC holder, which he won in 1916 at the Battle of Jutland. Both men are commemorated on plaques in St. Peter's Church].

Among the variety of leisure pursuits on offer in Edwardian times, travelling circuses probably provided the most entertainment; they were held either in the meadow by the station [until recently, where the Focus store stood] or in Mr Mould's field near the Cottage Hospital. Bostock and Wombwell's Travelling Menagerie came to Petersfield in 1909, 12 years after their previous visit, boasting numerous "carriages" containing lions, tigers, leopards, bears, hyenas, wolves, jaguars, monkeys, exotic birds,

Travelling circus advert

Bostock and Wombwell's menagerie

Tasmanian devils (marsupials), wild boars, and a white kangaroo. Children could ride on elephants, camels and dromedaries, and a military band played throughout the day. Fossett's Travelling Circus, Hippodrome and Menagerie, which had been in business for almost a century, twice came to Petersfield in the Edwardian era: they were famed for their Arab Troupe, expert horsemen and fifteen clowns.

Bathing in the Pond was popular, too, although there were qualms about nude bathers in the summer months! In the winter, hundreds of people took advantage of the frozen Pond to skate and slide on it. The mercury sank to 20 degrees below freezing on occasions, particularly with a stiff east wind blowing. This voluntary risk-taking, however, worried Town Councillors who felt that someone should be put in charge on days when there were crowds of skaters; life-saving equipment had been purchased, but it was not always easily available for use. A recent Public Health Act had given power to councils to close a pond during times of frost, and to charge admission, but only on condition that at least three quarters of the ice available for skating was open to the public free of charge.

In 1907, the Heath Committee of the UDC received a request from Mr Luker, one of the councillors, that they might consider allowing boats to be hired on the Pond, in order to produce some income. However, there still seemed to be some doubt as to the wisdom of attempting to purchase the rights (from the Lord of the Manor) to such facilities as the Heath and Pond could drain a considerable amount of money from the Council.

Among the sports available to local people in Petersfield, almost exclusively for men, were football, cricket, cycling, shooting, bowls and gymnastics.

A new Rifle Club was founded in 1906 and, given its natural military link, the number of recruits to the 3rd Volunteer Brigade of the Hants Regiment at the Drill Hall in Dragon Street [now The Maltings] had reached 33, bringing the total membership to 120, of which 90 attended the regimental camp. One of the favourite pastimes for men in these years was the annual shooting competition held on Butser every November and local shooting clubs were run by the Hants Carabiniers Yeomanry.

The Petersfield and District Bowls Club was founded in 1910. Bowls was played on ground offered by Mr Seymour Powell in St. Peter's Road, where the Club's Headquarters still stands.

BATHING IN THE HEATH POND :—
A PROTEST.

SIR,—I feel certain the majority of your readers will agree with me that it is quite time the bathers in the Heath Pond were compelled to wear bathing drawers. The present practice of bathers absolutely nude running from one end of the promenade to the other (in just the pleasantest part of the evening when one can enjoy a walk round the pond,) is a most indecent one, not tolerated in other towns and not conducive to good morals in our rising generation. Might I suggest that our Town Council take the matter up. It would be appreciated by many I am sure, as I frequently hear remarks of disgust expressed at the practice.—Yours &c.,   INHABITANT.
    Petersfield,
      8th July, 1901.

Protest letter about nude bathing

The Honorary Secretary of the Football Club, Frank Carpenter, in accepting his re-nomination for the post, remarked that they were "within measurable distance of obtaining a private ground" for the club. The ground mentioned was in Love Lane, but it was shortly to be taken over by the Petersfield builder, William Mould. However, terms were arranged with him to let the two pitches on that ground to the club for two afternoons a week and the use of a lock-up shed for a changing room. Meanwhile, Mr Lothian Bonham-Carter promised a donation towards the fees if it meant that football would no longer be played on the Heath ("the great thing would be to keep football off the Heath for the sake of cricket"). The Committee were left with the task of arranging a joint tenancy with the Dragons Club, the other football club in the town at that time.

Love Lane was the venue for the first ever six-a-side tournament which took place on Easter Monday, 1908. It attracted 900 spectators and profits were donated to the Cottage Hospital. The separate winding up of the two football clubs in the town took place in 1910, and the new combined club (Petersfield United Football Club) was formed at the end of the 1910 season.

A book published in the Edwardian era called A *Peep into the Past*, by F.H. Ayres, stated that cricket did not originate in Hambledon, as some had supposed until then, but in Surrey; however, it was certain that the Hambledon Club, and its Headquarters at the "Bat and Ball" Inn, was the first properly formed cricket club in the early 18th century of which there was any record and its members were rightly regarded as the pioneers of the game. Hambledon claimed a special distinction for one of its members, John Small senior, who, in 1775, was the first to score a century. John Small was from a noted Petersfield family who lived at no. 8 The Square [now

Saks Hair Salon]; his occupation is listed as that of cordwainer (shoemaker) as well as a cricket ball maker. His tombstone still stands in St. Peter's churchyard.

In 1908, a historic revival of the Hambledon v. All England match took place on Broadhalfpenny Down. For many years prior to 1777, this match was an annual fixture but was discontinued that year, although cricket was still played there. The idea of its revival was C.B. Fry's – and the old rules were obeyed, but it was played in modern dress. Fry was born in 1872 and was an outstanding athlete (playing cricket and football for England), but also a diplomat, politician, teacher and writer. He played cricket for Hampshire for 12 years from 1909, edited the Edwardian sports magazine, the C.B. Fry's Magazine, and played for Southampton in the F.A. Cup Final in 1902.

John Small's tombstone in the churchyard

This was also the occasion for the unveiling of a commemorative stone on the Down where the first contest had taken place – and when Hambledon beat England by an innings and 168 runs. In the revival match of 1908, Hambledon won by 4 wickets.

Cycling was *à la mode* in the Edwardian era and facilities for cyclists to stay overnight in the town were available at the Old Drum Inn (their slogan: "Ye Olde Drum – cannot be beaten") and the Temperance Hotel in the Square, the latter also serving as a restaurant and coffee tavern, where there was "excellent accommodation for commercials and cyclists".

A Volunteer Cyclist Corps was set up in the town in 1901. Volunteer cyclist units had started in the late 1880s and formed part of the British Army as specialist units

Petersfield Cycle Works

for reconnaissance, marksmanship, signalling and communication work. In 1908, they became reorganised and integrated into the Territorial Force by Secretary of State for War, Sir Richard Haldane, forming their own county battalions. They served as active units of the Army in the First World War and served abroad in many theatres of war, attached to the traditional infantry battalions. They eventually became the Territorial Army in 1920.

While the football teams had merged and the Bowls Club had been founded in 1910, the old Athletic Club – effectively a gymnastics club which had ceased to function in 1902 – was also revived. Certain athletic apparatus – a vaulting horse and springboard, for

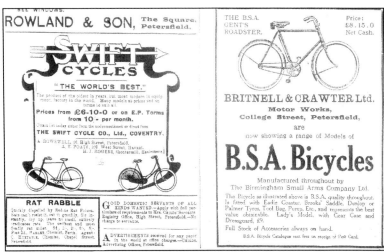

Cycle adverts

example – still existed in the Drill Hall, where a sergeant-instructor in gymnastics could be hired to coach newcomers. A list of some 40 potential members was produced and it was decided to go ahead and re-form the group.

One unusual pastime was that of competitive walking. Though it had been for several years an almost random exercise, by 1903 it had become a well-organised and extensively popular competition, which created much interest and excitement in the town and gave genuine pleasure to a good number of people. "Pedestrianism" brought out the crowds throughout the country and the Petersfield men who participated had to walk from the Dolphin Hotel in the High Street to the Angel Inn in Midhurst and back again, a distance of about 20 miles, which the winners achieved in just under 8 hours. There were 32 competitors in 1903 and the walkers were accompanied along the way by scores of cyclists and boys on foot. The press remarked that "a man 60 years of age who could walk to Midhurst and back at the rate of nearly 5 miles an hour showed that they had some very good men in Petersfield". A lad of 15 almost completed the course, but sadly was obliged to

Racewalking

abandon the event at Sheet on the way back. He was awarded a special prize by the organisers for his pluck.

A young man of 22, by the name of C.W. Allen and weighing only 8st. 3lbs, achieved a remarkable feat the same year: he had recently broken all world walking records for 1,000 and 2,000 miles and was the holder of the Lands' End to John-o-Groats and back record. He came to Petersfield to give an exhibition walk and naturally attracted much attention: starting from the Square soon after 5.30 p.m., he walked to Liss and back and covered the 10 miles in 1 hour and 10 minutes. He was accompanied by a number of cyclists "to whom his speed was a perfect revelation" and a collection was made on his behalf. Unlike most athletes, he did not believe in severe training, but rather favoured a natural diet; he advocated total abstinence from alcohol for all athletes.

Race-walking first appeared in the modern Olympics that year (1904) as a half-mile walk in the 'all-rounder,' the precursor to the 10-event decathlon. In 1908, stand-alone 1,500m and 3,000m race-walks were added and it is now an Olympic event with distances of 20 kilometres for both men and women and 50 kilometres for men only.

A local Olympian

In 1905, Petersfield had its own source of pride in an Olympic athlete: Lieut. Wyndham Halswelle, the son of Keeley and Helen Halswelle of Stoner House, Steep, became the quarter mile champion of England (his country of birth) and Scotland (by virtue of his being a member of Edinburgh Harriers). The following year, he ran in the "intercalated" Olympic games in Athens, which were attended by King Edward and Queen Alexandra. These "intercalated games" were held midway between the Olympiads of 1904 and 1908 and took place at the Panathinaiko Stadium. They were an international multi-sport event considered to be at the time a true Olympiad and sometimes referred to as the "Second International Olympic Games in Athens", but, although medals were distributed, they are no longer recognised by the International Olympic Committee. They did, however, create a lasting, multiple legacy for the Olympic Movement: they held separate Opening and Closing Ceremonies, the athletes marched into the stadium in national teams, each following its national flag – which was raised for the winning athletes in each discipline – and an Olympic village was created to house the athletes.

Wyndham Halswelle

Born in 1882, Wyndham Halswelle had been educated at Castle House School in the Square, and then at Charterhouse School. He spent one year at the Royal Military Academy, Sandhurst, and was commissioned as a 2nd lieutenant in 1901. A year later, he was gazetted to the 2nd Highland Light Infantry and drafted to South Africa to fight in the Boer War.

At the "intercalated" Olympics, Halswelle won a silver medal for the 400m (his only defeat at this distance) and a bronze medal for the 800m. Two years later, at the London Olympics, he won the gold medal for the 400 metres on the newly-constructed White City track. It was the only Olympic "walkover" (that is, a single runner with no opponents) in history and it provoked a diplomatic incident with the USA. Several accounts of the incident have been published, but Halswelle's own diary recorded the following :

The Olympic Stadium, 1906

"When we lined up for the final, we were warned that any boring or fouling would immediately disqualify the perpetrator. I had drawn no.1 (i.e. inside position) in both my heats, and was unfortunate in drawing 2 in the final. Judges were placed about every 40 yards round the track, I suppose in view of my treatment in Athens (i.e. in 1906, when he was also the victim of "boxing" and jostling).

We got off to a fair start. I was running 2nd after about 30 yards when Robbins on my right cut in across me, I think in an unfair manner, as he had not the proper clearance to do it. I dropped my stride just a little. I was very careful to avoid being pocketed, with one in front and one on my right.

When we neared the last corner, with about 120 yards to go, it flashed through my mind that if I got a 5 yard lead, it would be toss-up if they would ever catch me again. I accordingly made my effort. Carpenter was then on the inside, certainly not more than 2 feet from the curb. As I attempted to pass him, he put his right elbow across my chest and, as I moved out to get past him, he did likewise, boring me about 14 feet across the track.

I first noticed the booing of the crowd at the corner, and then saw, when about 80 or 90 yards from the tape, the judges break the tape and hold up their hands. I did *not run myself out and Carpenter crossed the line about a yard or so ahead of me.*

About an hour afterwards, there were still some 20,000 people waiting to hear the result of the enquiry, which was held in the Garden Club. I had to attend, but was not required to say anything as Carpenter was not present."

[*reproduced by permission of Halswelle's biographer, Michael Stewart, 2006*]

At the enquiry, the race was declared void and the officials ordered a re-run two days later, in lanes, without Carpenter. However, the other two American runners refused to race under these conditions and, although reluctant to do so, Halswelle ran the 400m again by himself, in a time of 50.2 s. It was the only time in Olympic history where the final has been a "walk-over" and, as a result of the controversy, from the next Olympics onwards, all 400m races were run in lanes and the International Amateur Athletic Federation was founded to establish uniform, worldwide rules for athletics.

Halswelle's Olympic gold medal

Halswelle's army career took him next to Ireland; he was promoted to Captain at the age of 29 and posted to the 1st Highland Light Infantry. In 1911, the battalion was sent to India, where it was based at Lucknow. He returned to England the following year and continued to move around the country frequently until Britain declared war on Germany in August 1914. For the first three months of the war, he was stationed first at Portsdown, then at Gosport, before being shipped over to France in January 1915. He was killed by sniper fire at Neuve Chapelle two months later, at the age of 32.

Public Utilities and services

(i) WATER:

The question of whether to invest in a new filtration system to provide clearer water for the town, free from iron, was still exercising the UDC in 1901. The cost of a deeper borehole to provide better quality water was ruled out as too expensive and the example of Farnham was quoted to demonstrate the advantages of filtration for the town.

Much debate took place around this time (1902) on the question of street watering. A new water cart was to be bought for the town to help keep the streets dust-free. The UDC did not, however, go so far as to provide a combined road sweeper and sprinkler and a refuse cart for household waste, as some residents had requested.

One shopkeeper complained that dust came into his shop early in the mornings and that an early watering – say, between 5 a.m. and 6 a.m. – and an attention to watering the kerbs and pavements too, would alleviate this problem.

Street hydrants provided water for street watering, but the supply was finite and, in times of drought, there was a danger that the town's supply would run out. It had been thought that pumping water from the town streams was possible, but that would incur more expense, so the decision to water the streets or not had had to be left to Mr H.T. Keates (the architect and UDC councillor on the Water Committee). The problem of supply was alleviated in 1909 when a new source was obtained for the town at Hawkley. Negotiations had been underway for some time with the owner of the land – Sir John Hutchinson – at Oakshott Farm, where the springs were sufficiently high to enable the water to be brought to the existing reservoir by gravitation and thus save all the expense of pumping. The quality of the water was also very pure and it would not require filtration; the quantity available, roughly 150,000 gallons per day, would be amply sufficient to supply the town's needs. The UDC purchased the site – about 138 acres in total – which included 50 acres of hop land, a farmhouse and outbuildings, and five cottages, for £5,100.

(ii) Gas:

After much deliberation and debate, both in the local UDC and, nationally, in the House of Commons – under the provisions of the Petersfield and Selsey Gas Act of 1901 – the old Petersfield Gas, Coke and Oil Company and the Selsey Gas and Lighting Company received the Royal Assent to merge and became the Petersfield and Selsey Gas Company.

The old Company had been constituted in 1851 but the gas supply was now inadequate for the expanding populations of the two areas, so the

The Hylton Road gasworks (centre right of picture)

new parliamentary powers obtained by the new Company allowed them to increase their supply to small consumers in both areas. Joint management for the two areas would result in economies of scale and greater management efficiency.

The new gasworks in Hylton Road were opened in 1902.

(III) TELEPHONES:

In 1902, a request was made to the UDC, strongly backed by local businesses, to have the town connected to the telephone. The Postmaster General apparently had it under consideration, but the decision depended on the town having a viable number of subscribers. Four years later, the UDC again applied to the General Post Office for a telephone exchange in Petersfield, especially as a trunk line would enable direct contact with London to be made.

An effort had also been made to get a small, purely local, connection between the Isolation Hospital, Union Workhouse, Cottage Hospital, and two or three other specified places in case of emergency, but this had fallen through because they were told that no private wire could be used at the Post Office. All the local villages close to Petersfield were connected to the Post Office by telephone and the UDC was sure that many residents of the town would become subscribers.

At last, in 1907, the Post Office central call office achieved communication with all trunk lines and, a year later, there were 37 telephones in the town, the vast majority of them owned by businesses. Their numbers were published in the *Hants and Sussex News*.

(IV) SANITATION:

In 1903, the UDC spent a great deal of time discussing the defective sanitation in many houses in the town, principally those owned by Lord Hylton. The "Inspector of Nuisances", Mr Keates, had already called for certain sanitary defects at houses in Sheep Street and North Road to be remedied. An example of the kind of problems which occurred at this time was the report that, at one property in Sheep Street, three cases of diphtheria had occurred and there was no ventilation to the toilet; at five other houses in the same street, also owned by Lord

Sheep Street

Hylton, there were only three privies (earth closets). The UDC decided that, if there was a continual recurrence of the nuisance, then the owners would be compelled to connect the property to the drains.

The town's health was the subject of annual reports by the Medical Officer of Health – in Edwardian times, this was Dr. H.M. Brownfield – and these were presented to the UDC for comment. Petersfield's birth rate for 1909 stood at 20.4 per thousand, an exceedingly low figure (although, nationally, the birth rate had declined almost uninterruptedly since 1876 and was exceptionally low in Sussex, Surrey, Devonshire and Hampshire). The rate was even lower the following year; in fact, the lowest for 30 years. However, the death rate was also extremely low and compared favourably with that of the whole county. Periodical inspections were carried out in schools, dairies, bakehouses and slaughterhouses and, with a few minor exceptions, these were deemed to be clean and sanitary. The town's refuse disposal "required attention" in 1909, since it was mostly deposited in a field on the road to Sheet, some distance, however, from any dwelling house. A correspondent to the local press complained of the failure to disinfect the town's drains "which are at times very offensive".

(V) ELECTRIC LIGHTING:

Notice was given to the UDC in 1907 that a private individual was applying for a provisional Electric Lighting Order for the Petersfield District which would also cover the parishes of Liss, Steep and Sheet. An irate letter to the *Hants and Sussex News* in 1908 deplored the abominable state of lighting in the town and called for the adoption of electric lighting in place of the gas lighting which prevailed at the time.

A proposal to install electric lighting in Petersfield was made by Messrs Edwards and Armstrong in 1910, if the UDC would agree to their conditions, viz. to allow the company to break up the streets to begin the installation at once; to agree to support the company in the future if they applied for a provisional lighting order; to allow the company to use overhead wires (except in the main

> ## "LIGHT, MORE LIGHT!"
>
> SIR,—When some few years since a prominent townsman advocated the adoption of electric lighting for the town, he met with a torrent of expostulation and wild abuse.
>
> At the present time, doubtless, most of those who formerly scoffed are of my opinion—that almost any form of lighting would be preferable to that which we now *enjoy* in Petersfield. To call the commodity "gas" is a libel, pure and simple. The streets are badly lighted, the shops are pretty well as bad, whilst in the places of worship the light supplied is simply abominable.
>
> But even this wretched "luminant" has one saving grace —— its aroma! Ye gods, isn't it sublime! Yet, sir, we are charged 4s. 8d. per thousand for this apology for light.
>
> In no other business concern in the town is such poor value given for money—yet we *must* buy this stuff, or, at considerable expense, re-arrange our lighting. How long are we to put up with this palpable injustice?—
> Yours, etc.,
> OLD GOLD.

*"Light – more light!" letter,*1908

streets) at 350 volts; and to agree to a provision of lighting for a period of 10-15 years. However, the UDC turned down this offer, as they could not see their way to giving these assurances.

(VI) POSTAL SERVICES:

Mr W.C. Burley, Chairman of the UDC, speaking in the new Council chamber in 1907, reminisced about the improved public services in the town since he had first become Council Clerk in the 1870s. In those days, the work of the Post Office was carried out by two ladies assisted by two postmen for the sorting. One man covered the delivery throughout the town and he had to find other work to fill his time: he was also the caretaker at the Corn Exchange and a billposter. There were now 30 postal workers in the town. Similarly, when he had started work, the mail was delivered by pony and cart;

Edwardian letter box in Station Road

in 1907, there were the beginnings of a motor delivery service and altogether 12,000 letters were now being delivered weekly. Petersfield was considered to be the most important postal centre for a rural district in the District Surveyor's area.

Road and rail improvements

Some indication of the development in transport, and therefore in people's mobility, can be seen in the improvements to, and consequent advertisements for, road and rail transport.

Interestingly, it was with some considerable foresight that proposals for an extension to the railway station were debated as early as 1901: at a meeting between the UDC and the London and South Western Railway Company, it was pointed out to the latter that the town was likely to develop immensely in the near future. In the Edwardian era, there were in fact only two small roads to the north-west of the railway line: Penns Road (built for railway workers in Victorian times) and Rushes Road (constructed, with the first tranche of houses, in 1898). There were clear signs that this section of the town – a sort of "West Petersfield" – would accommodate a great deal of expansion, although this possibility was only to be exploited much later with the development of the Bell Hill estate in the 1930s. Thus, the town, which had until the arrival of the railway been centred around the historic Market Square, developed slowly in Victorian times towards the railway line to the north-west of the town. (It remains to be seen when the next expansion – to the latest man-made boundary, the by-pass – will be effected.)

As for the railway, it was suggested that the Company might consider building a new station on the London side of the crossing, which would obviate the Midhurst trains going over the crossing at all. One effect of this proposal would be to separate the passenger traffic (on the London side) from the goods traffic (to remain on the Portsmouth side for shunting and deliveries). As it transpired, this separation was not accepted by the L & SWR, but some of the station's inconveniences were addressed.

Complaints received about the level crossing, for example, were partially met by the lengthening and widening of the down platform, the addition of a loop line through the station on the up side, and the construction of an island platform with convenient waiting rooms on the up side. The public road underbridge, south of the station, was also widened and improved and additional sidings and goods accommodation included in the scheme.

The whole scheme took 18 months to complete in 1901-2 and not only improved the railwaymen's task of shunting, but also afforded passengers greater convenience and comfort in their journeys. With a view to preventing delays for vehicles at the level crossing, the Railway Company had provided the long siding for goods traffic on the Portsmouth side of the station; the signal box was extended to house new equipment; a signal box at "the Rushes" bridge [now Frenchman's Road] was replaced by a ground box and the road under the bridge widened to help traffic; longer platforms were built to accommodate longer trains; and new platforms were built to serve the branch line to Midhurst

Petersfield Station in Edwardian times

and avoid interfering with the main line traffic. The up goods yard was extended to provide space for the incoming and outgoing milk lorries to operate; these were now able to drive directly up to the loading bays and save manual labour in transferring the churns.

The credit for bringing about all these improvements was entirely due to Mr Way, the stationmaster.

The level crossing was still causing fears of an accident and a particularly horrendous one was recorded in 1902, when a long-serving railwayman, having waited by the signal box for a down train to pass, started to cross the line and was instantly knocked down by an express up train which he had neither seen nor heard. In 1906, the L & SWR threatened to close the right of way over the crossing to all pedestrians. The history of this extraordinary decision went back 18 months, when the railway company, without any notice, had decided to block the pedestrian way across the tracks via a wicket gate near the main gates. It was believed at the time that this decision had been made due to the extra work entailed opening and shutting the wicket gates from the signal box. It was intended that the signalman would only open the gates when a cycle, carriage or motor was seen waiting to go through. Subsequently, the railway company had placed a Bill before Parliament which would have enshrined the decision in law and it was pure chance that the local authority had heard of it. The UDC were authorised to oppose the Bill before Parliament. The problem was resolved a few weeks later, when the company agreed to re-site the wicket gate immediately next to the main gates.

Under the provisions of the Private Street Works Act of 1892, Durford Road was able to obtain new sewering and levelling as a private road in 1902, although the owners of properties had to be charged (via the rates) for a certain percentage of the costs. However, the residents objected to the scheme and the case went before the Magistrates' Court, where the objection was quashed.

There were further extensive roadworks carried out in 1904: the High Street was newly paved, Station Road and Chapel Street were widened and the corner building [now Coral] brought out further across the pavement; and Hylton Road was tarred and Lavant Street, Chapel Street and Heath Road were also paved in 1908.

With the increase in traffic as the years passed, there was, naturally, a corresponding increase in road accidents: 1904 saw two particularly bad smashes, luckily without great personal injury. Mr Charles Cave's bus collided with a motor car at the Dragon Street / Hylton Road corner, with considerable damage to both vehicles. Earlier the same week, two motorcycles collided at the bottom of the High Street by the Red Lion, both drivers being thrown from their machines but not seriously injured.

1910 motorcycle

Childs' timetable – published on behalf of the L & SWR by A.W. Child's printing office in the High Street – shows the frequency and cost of travel to London and Portsmouth in 1909. There were three classes of travel, the first-class fare being roughly twice the cost of the third class; trains stopped at Weybridge, Surbiton and Wimbledon; cheap day returns were available on Thursdays (the first-class fare was 14/6d and the third class 7/6d); other cheap returns were available on various days to Virginia Water, Windsor and Eton, Guildford, Hayling Island and the Isle of Wight. As can be seen from the timetable, the journey to London took a minimum of 2 hours on an ordinary train, and 1hr 20 minutes on the express service; and excursions to London

CHILDS' TIME TABLE. 1st June, 1909, to 30th September, 1909.

£. & S.W.R. Portsmouth Direct Line.

Childs' timetable, 1909

for Harrod's Sale Week (heralded as "The greatest Shopping Event of the Year") were advertised in the *Hants and Sussex News* every summer and cost just 3/- (three shillings) for a third-class return.

Harrods Sale Week, 1909

For those who were looking further afield, there were excursions to Normandy in the summer of 1910, offering the chance to enjoy the *fêtes* of every description, aviation and race meetings, regattas, tennis tournaments and golf competitions and the resorts of Trouville, Cabourg and Etretat. Given the unusually large number of visitors expected and the availability of both night and daytime services, it is clear that Petersfield was part of the railway's target audience, particularly since its population appeared to include many who were able to afford these luxuries.

London, 1909

Social and Technological Progress

The Edwardian era was characterised by a remarkable advance in technology and its associated human comforts. It was the decade of the motor car and the first aeroplanes, of the development of the wireless and the telephone, and of the first electric lighting in the streets, coinciding with the first public transport.

In a letter to the press in 1906, the Headmaster of Churcher's College, the Rev W. Henry Bond, had called for better electric lighting in Petersfield's streets and shops, telephones, electric cars, the removal of the railway crossing and the abolition of "unwholesome stenches" in the town. In fact, the problems with the town's lighting and the railway level crossing were to remain contentious for many years, but cars were already in evidence and the telephone exchange was established in 1907.

THE AUTO-HIPPIQUE.

Some idea of the recent inventions and new-fangled machinery available to the public can be seen in the advertisements in the press at this time: the "auto-hippique" and the "tricar" appeared in 1906, for example. In the air, hot-air balloons were the latest craze to create excitement among the public: a balloon appeared over Petersfield in 1905, one of three in a race which had started from the Crystal Palace earlier. It belonged to the Aero Club and, after a flight of over two hours, landed on the South Downs.

By September 1911, the distinction between pleasure flights and the military use

THE TRICAR.

of aircraft was undoubtedly becoming blurred: the aviator who passed over Petersfield one Sunday evening in an Army Bristol biplane was in fact visiting his home at Tillington, near Petworth. He was Lieutenant Basil Barrington-Kennett, an officer in the Grenadier Guards, but attached to the Aerial Corps for a period of three years. He had taken off from Salisbury Plain early that morning, but encountered thick mist and crosswinds, and so landed near Hambledon, where his machine was visited by hundreds of people.

When the weather improved, he set off again and reached his home later in the evening.

Bristol biplane

Towards the end of the Edwardian era, the electrical industry was heralding the advent of metallic filament lamps instead of carbon filaments. The initial antagonism towards this innovation was quickly dispelled as consumers realised that they were using far less electricity than before. Electricity was beginning to replace gas as the preferred (and cheaper) option for all types of lighting. It also had the benefit of being cleaner, and therefore healthier, especially for home lighting. For street lighting, several large city corporations were already experimenting with electricity and saving ratepayers money.

Human endeavour also progressed rapidly in the Edwardian era and aroused the interest of the population at large. Its social reach encompassed, for example, the rapid expansion of the Scout Movement (see page 73), the advancement of the Suffragettes' campaigns, and, on an international scale, the polar expeditions of Scott and Shackleton.

The Suffragette Movement, although derived intellectually from such advocates as John Stuart Mill in the mid-nineteenth century, came into its own politically when, first, Millicent Fawcett in 1897 and, second, Emmeline Pankhurst in 1903, founded their respective organisations: the National Union of Women's Suffrage Societies and the National Women's Social and Political Union (NWSPU). Real radical – and militant – campaigning began and ended with Pankhurst in the period immediately before the First World War.

Emmeline Pankhurst

The Suffragette movement brought about much public debate locally: Emmeline Pankhurst had been invited by Mrs Badley to give a lecture at Bedales in 1907, where her politically radical ideas found sympathy and some support. After an analysis of the historical background to the women's movement over the previous 50 years, and justifying all the tactics which had been used so far in their campaigning, she concluded by alluding to the social, physical and moral degradation which so many women had to suffer because they could not earn enough to live decently and honestly. She appealed to every woman and every right minded man to help women obtain that political equality so urgently needed. Mrs Pankhurst explained that women's opposition to the recently elected Liberal government, which had won a landslide victory in 1906 under Henry Campbell-Bannerman, was only to last as long as the Party refused to introduce a measure to give women the vote on the same terms as it had been given to men.

At a highly successful "Votes for Women" public meeting held a few months later in the Corn Exchange organised by the NWSPU, there was a large proportion of women – though not a majority – present, and, when it came to voting on the resolution submitted ("This meeting calls upon the Government to grant facilities for the discussion of the Bill for the Enfranchisement of Women now before the House"), it was clear that the majority of the audience sympathised with the objectives of the Women's Movement, several of whom had spoken at the meeting.

History subsequently saw women in the UK given the vote in 1918 if they were over 30 and met certain property qualifications. In 1928, suffrage was extended to all women over the age of 21.

WSPU *Votes for Women poster*, 1909

As far as work for women was concerned, the Petersfield Women's Institute held an interesting meeting in 1903, at which various speakers made suggestions as to how women might be trained for, and employed in, schoolteaching, Post Office work or laundry work. Redolent of the Victorian legacy of ethically-sound and life-enhancing opportunities for women, the debate contemplated the possibility that, by undertaking the last of these trades, "educated women should qualify as manageresses of public laundries for the sake of the good influence they might exert, while at the same time earning a livelihood for themselves". The debate concluded with a discussion as to whether women and the country in general were benefited by the increasing opportunities for women in the workplace. Countering this, another speaker pointed out some of the dangers and drawbacks of a business life and urged the cultivation of domestic virtues.

The East Hants Liberal Women's Association held a meeting in 1905 to hear Miss Emma Wood speak on the topic of "The Evolution of Women's Work". Mrs Hester Money-Coutts, presiding, opened the meeting by remarking that this was probably not the moment to ask the leading question: how far might women legitimately take part in politics? However, she did state her view that the current Tory government, by their reckless expenditure and increased taxation, had made politics a matter of as great importance to women as to men. The speaker began by outlining the changes in the position, opportunities and privileges of women during the Victorian era: the introduction of machinery, Victorian inventions and the consequent creation of the great middle classes had had a marvellous effect in lightening the domestic labours of women. The dilemma – and injustice – for women was that occupations which were at one time regarded as exclusively women's had come to be absorbed by men, yet any effort on the part of women to enter fields of action or remunerative employment which, through custom, had become looked upon as men's prerogative and right, had produced a storm of opposition. It was beginning to be acknowledged that women's vocation in life, as well as men's, was work; they were no longer dependent on the exertions of men for a living; their own energies in the household had decreased considerably thanks to new labour-saving devices; they no longer saw marriage as the ultimate goal in life; they could now accept that they could be the breadwinners for others.

There was a lamentable dearth of occupations for women at this time, and, apart from the "spheres of usefulness" such as teaching and nursing (thanks largely to the respective efforts of Frances Mary Buss and Florence Nightingale), the development of the Women's Movement in Victorian times had resulted in better education for women; furthermore, the establishment of the Primrose League in 1883 (formed to promote Toryism across Great Britain) and the Women's Liberal Federation in 1887 had steadily increased the power of women in society. What the speaker now called for was the opening of one branch of politics – Local Government – to women and the plight of hundreds of thousands of women factory workers, who often still worked in appalling conditions.

This meeting's Chairman, Mrs Money-Coutts, lived at Stodham Park in East Liss and was President of the East Hants Division of the Liberal Social Council. She was the wife of Hugh Burdett Money-Coutts, who was the unsuccessful Liberal candidate in the East Hants constituency at the general election a few months later in January 1906. In the 1880s, she had donated to the town a drinking trough for cattle at the market and it stood in front of the Coffee Tavern [now the site of Petersfield Library, but the trough stands in front of Rhona Russell] and had donated sufficient money to keep the trough clean and filled with water. The Money-Coutts moved with their three children to Devon in 1908.

Drinking trough donated by Mrs Money-Coutts

The Edwardian era witnessed a burst of activity in the field of polar exploration: what came to be termed "The Heroic Age of Antarctic Exploration" began with the British National Antarctic Expedition of 1901–1904, led by Captain Robert Falcon Scott in his ship *Discovery*, which came to within 463 nautical miles of the South Pole from its base at McMurdo Sound.

The British Expedition of 1907–09, otherwise known as the *Nimrod* Expedition, was the first of three expeditions to the Antarctic led by Ernest Shackleton, who had been Third Officer on Scott's team three years earlier. Its main target, among a range of geographical and scientific objectives, was to be first to reach the South Pole. This was not attained, but the expedition's southern march reached just 97 nautical miles from the Pole, before having to turn back.

The Norwegian, Roald Amundsen, was the first to reach the South Pole in December 1911 from his ship *Fram*. He was followed by Scott from the *Terra Nova* over a month later, using the route pioneered by Shackleton. Most of us are familiar with the tragic circumstances of the deaths of Scott's party on the return journey after being delayed by a series of accidents, bad weather and the declining physical condition of the men.

The *Imperial Trans-Antarctic Expedition* of 1914, led by Ernest Shackleton, set out to cross the continent via the Pole, but their ship, the *Endurance*, was trapped and crushed by pack ice before they even landed. The expedition members survived after an epic journey on sledges over pack ice to Elephant Island.

Local interest in all this remarkable human endeavour centred first around an appeal in 1902 by the mother of Lieutenant C. Rawson Royds, who had accompanied Scott as First Lieutenant on his first expedition in the *Discovery*. The Royds had lived in Petersfield before moving to Havant. The funds were being sought for a relief

ship to be sent out in the summer of 1902 to render assistance to Scott and his party. The relief mission – to free the *Discovery* from pack ice – was accomplished and the return home was hailed as a success, although questions remained about the ability to master the techniques of efficient polar travel using skis and dogs, a legacy which persisted in British Antarctic Expeditions throughout the Heroic Age.

Shackleton's Nimrod crew at Cape Royds

Royds had been a pupil at Eastman's School in Southsea before becoming a naval cadet in 1892 and a career Royal Navy officer; as one of Scott's officers, Cape Royds in Antarctica was named after him. On the expedition's return in 1904, Royds gave a lecture on his experiences in the Corn Exchange in Petersfield. Throughout WW1, he commanded the battleship HMS *Emperor of India*; after retirement from the Navy as a Rear Admiral, he served as Deputy Commissioner of the London Metropolitan Police; after a further promotion to Vice Admiral, he died suddenly whilst in office as Assistant Police Commissioner in 1931.

Petersfield's second Polar connection came about in 1910, when Dr. Harry Roberts, the London G.P. who had settled on Oakshott Hanger two years earlier, brought his family down from London to take up permanent residence in Hampshire.

His 18-year old daughter Hazel had met her future husband, George Marston, at her father's Stepney house, where he had been invited to dinner by Harry Roberts' art lecturer friend, Winifred Stamp. Marston missed his train home, stayed the night, then, six months later, married Hazel.

Marston had been Shackleton's official artist on the Nimrod expedition of 1907-9 and he now took up the simple life in residence at Oakshott with the little fraternity of the Roberts clan. He and Hazel lived first at Holdens Cottage on Oakshott Hanger, then

Dr Harry Roberts with George Marston at Oakshott Hanger

moved into The Folly, which Harry had built for them as a wedding present, close by his own house. Marston, described by Eleanor Farjeon as "plump, easy-going and very amusing", was the one person who could make Harry roar with laughter. His accounts and imitation of penguins at the South Pole soon earned him the nickname "Penguin" – an alternative sobriquet to "Muffin", the usual name given to him by friends and family. He and Hazel married in Kensington in 1913, but, from 1914 to 1916, Marston left with Shackleton on his second South Pole expedition in the *Endurance*. Later, he turned his hand to fruit farming at Oakshott, taught art at Bedales School and continued to sketch and paint in the neighbourhood of Steep. He and Hazel and their two children eventually drifted apart as a family.

On a more parochial scale, discoveries were being made by archaeologists in the Petersfield area: in May 1906, A. Moray Williams, a teacher at Bedales School, uncovered the site of a Romano-British villa at Stroud on farmland owned by Mr F. Bridger. A year later, he was able to announce to the press that a whole wing of the villa had been uncovered, containing about a dozen rooms, three of which were heated by hypocausts and one of which was still lined with large, unbroken "box tiles". Many floors were still visibly paved with *tesserae* [floor mosaics], and several coins of the late Empire period were found, showing that the house had been occupied in the 4th century A.D. The excavations had taken place thanks to donations

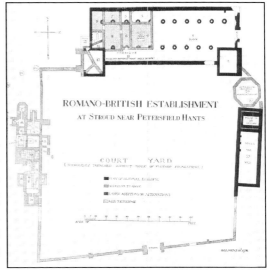

Plan of the Roman villa at Stroud

received from individuals and from the Society of Antiquaries, and the site was opened to the public in 1907. Sadly, by 1909, the income from donations had dried up and the digging had to stop – the whole site was covered with earth again to preserve it, a galling outcome to Moray Williams's dedication and a loss to the neighbourhood's heritage potential.

The excavated remains at Stroud

A little further afield and another site of interest to Moray Williams, the remains of a Roman courtyard and villa with mosaics and hypocausts had been uncovered at Lippen Wood, close to West Meon, in 1905. There were also remains of a bloomery nearby – a furnace for smelting iron.

Social change at this time was often stimulated by the greater or lesser generosity of the wealthiest in Petersfield society. A new operating theatre in the Cottage Hospital, for example, far in advance of many attached to much larger hospitals, was built thanks to the generosity of Mr John Bonham-Carter. The town benefited either through individual donations to just causes or through a process of public subscription which, encouraged by the press, accounted for the establishment of new institutions or buildings for the benefit of the whole community. Indeed, it appeared to be a relatively simple task to persuade the wealthier sections of the community to part with their money. For example, the vicar of St. Peter's, Canon Causton, set up a local Distress Fund and started a soup kitchen for the unemployed. The Oddfellows, a Friendly Society set up on a national scale to protect and care for its own members, met, like the Masons, in Lodges, and held annual fundraising dinners. In 1908, a "Shilling Shelter" fund was created for the purpose of providing a movable shelter for the cattle which were brought to market. Until that point, cattle had been subjected to the vagaries of the climate and this aroused much indignation among residents.

Adverts for Friendly Societies

Interestingly, there was at this time some concern nationally over the depopulation of rural areas, although it seems likely that Petersfield, still a relatively small country town, was seen more as a focus for its own rural area than as a magnet drawing countryfolk away from their rural occupations and pursuits. At a symposium on the subject in 1903, the Literary and Debating Society offered members the opportunity to present 5-minute papers on the topic; this resulted in a general consensus of opinion on the need for the decentralisation of manufactories – a phenomenon which had already begun in various parts of the country. Other suggestions for stemming the exodus from the land were: the nationalisation and municipalisation of the land, the creation of smallholdings and allotments, the abolition of "landlordism", the creation of "garden cities", better housing and fixity of tenure, the removal of class distinctions, more leisure and means of recreation, the establishment of village industries and handicrafts, schools of training, the nationalisation of the railways, and the setting up of village improvement societies. This list is instructive in that it outlines some of the social concerns of the Edwardian era generally.

As if to respond in a positive fashion to this litany of social gripes, the same Society invited Mr J. Richardson, the High Street bookseller, to speak on "Past and present in English villages, towns and cities". His talk to the Society ten years previously, entitled "The Possibilities of Petersfield", had shown a utopian view of the very desirable, but very distant town. Some of his ideas proposed at the time had now been realised: why, he now asked, should Petersfield in its future enlargement not aim to become a garden city? The town's advantages lay in its undulating surface, its wealth of verdure, its good drinking water, invigorating air and comparatively mild winters. He did not know of any residential towns which equalled the surrounding scenery of Petersfield. Its river, the Western Rother, was outside the town proper, but what the town had was very much better: its beautiful lake surrounded by the Heath. Over the past ten years, he continued, there had been some considerable improvements: better educational and travel facilities, opportunities for enjoyment and improved services to the "struggling masses".

Farmworkers were being targeted during the Edwardian era as potential emigrants to Canada and New Zealand. Canada was offering 160 acres free to British farmers ("Get your own farm"), while New Zealand ("The settler's ideal home") offered reduced fares to agricultural labourers, shepherds, wood cutters and men able to milk cows and manage livestock. Their wives, and other female applicants, were offered employment as domestic servants.

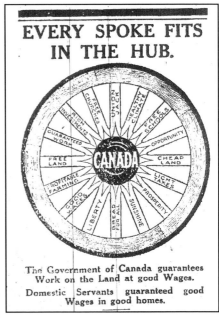

EVERY SPOKE FITS IN THE HUB.

The Government of Canada guarantees Work on the Land at good Wages.

Domestic Servants guaranteed good Wages in good homes.

Inducement to emigrate to Canada

Such examples as these indicate just how much and how widespread was the desire for change in the fabric of society. The government, keeping pace with such desires, came to the rescue of the most unfortunate in society and established the Pensions Act in 1908 and, three years later, instigated the National Insurance Act, covering provision for health and unemployment for the first time.

Enticement to New Zealand

Local and National Politics

The end of May 1902 marked the end of the Second Boer War in South Africa. It had begun in October 1899 and ended with the annexation of the independent republics of the Transvaal and the Orange Free State by the British Empire; both would eventually be incorporated in 1910 into the Union of South Africa, a dominion of the British Empire. In traditionally patriotic Petersfield, streets were spanned with strings of flags, and "few houses were without some token of the jubilation that prevailed". People paraded the streets, wearing bows of red, white and blue, while carts, perambulators and even horses and dogs were bedecked with flags and favours. The Town Crier was to the fore in a quasi-military costume to announce the news of the declaration of peace. Board School children were assembled in the Square and addressed by the vice-chairman of the School Board, Mr W.B. Edgeler, who told them they were to be given a half-day holiday that afternoon. The infants, who carried miniature Union Jacks, sang the action song "The Flag of England"; and the older pupils followed this with "Now pray we for our country" and "Soldiers of the King". The whole crowd which had collected then concluded with "God save the King". The evening saw a torchlight procession around the streets organised by the Working Men's Association, and church bells were rung to celebrate the glad tidings of victory.

Mr Thomas Summers, the Town Crier, was to die in 1907 after many years' service. The UDC voted to continue the tradition of having all notices cried and to provide a bell for the new crier, though not a cloak or a hat – or a horse! Harry Summers, a billposter, took over the role, but he died in 1908.

The year 1906 was memorable for the remarkable wave of Liberalism which swept through the country. In the General Election in January that year, the Conservatives under Balfour were roundly beaten by Campbell-Bannerman's Liberals, while the incipient Labour party was becoming ever more successful. In East Hants, the seat had swung from Liberal to Conservative in 1892, and the Liberal candidate in 1906 – H.B. Money-Coutts – was very unfortunate in only losing to Mr W.G. Nicholson by 96 votes out of a poll of 8,500. W.G. Nicholson had first been elected for the Conservatives in 1897; he was the son of William Nicholson of Basing Park, who had first held the seat in 1866, and his son was to maintain it throughout the Edwardian period, considerably extending his lead over the Liberals in 1910. Several political debates took place in Petersfield in 1908-9 on the emerging forces of Liberalism and

Socialism; over 500 people attended a meeting in the Corn Exchange, for example, to hear a debate on Free Trade and Tariff Reform (which had split the Conservative Party).

Previous election results in the East Hants constituency show how close the two parties generally were:

W.G. Nicholson and his supporters

```
1885 : Lord Wolmer (Liberal) .........................3414
       William Nicholson (Conservative).......3253
       Liberal majority.......................................161

1886 : Lord Wolmer (Liberal/Unionist)...........3188
       William Nicholson (Conservative).......3077
       Unionist majority .....................................111

1892 : William Wickham (Conservative).........3912
       J. Bonham-Carter (Liberal) ...................3008
       Conservative majority.............................904

1895 : William Wickham returned unopposed

1897 : W.G. Nicholson (Conservative).............3748
       J. Bonham-Carter (Liberal) ...................3328
       Conservative majority.............................420

1900 : Mr W.G. Nicholson returned unopposed
```

Such was Mr Nicholson's popularity that he easily won the next contest, in 1910, against the new Liberal candidate, H. Arthur Baker, by a margin of 2,685 votes. Indeed, Hampshire was moving overwhelmingly in the direction of the Conservatives at this point, although in East Hants it was also obvious that the newcomer, Mr Baker – a stranger to the community – was hardly likely to unseat an opponent who had been building roots here for the previous 12 years, was keenly interested in agriculture,

DAINTY COTTON FROCKS FOR SUMMER WEAR.

A FASHIONABLE BATHING GOWN.

CORSELET BOLERO COSTUME.

AN OVERALL FOR SCHOOL.

COSTUME FOR BUSINESS GIRL.

Smart and useful Hat in Grey Straw, trimmed shaded Pink to Grey Roses and Foliage, only 10/6.

Edwardian Fashions

had been President of the Hampshire County Cricket Club, was a Hampshire magistrate and commanded the 3rd Battalion Hampshire Regiment. On policy matters, local M.P.s, such as Nicholson, and the Prime Minister, Arthur Bonar Law, benefited from the popularity of Tariff Reform. This measure – an element of protectionism for a producing country like Britain – was introduced partly to pay for

The 1910 election winner in St. Peter's Road

the Boer War and partly to reduce the costs of Free Trade which had been in effect since the 1870s.

In local politics, the UDC lost its Chairman of nine years' standing, Mr W.B. Edgeler, in 1902. The other members of the Council were Messrs R.G. Cross, W.C. Burley, F.C. Cox, A. Johnson, H.M. Brownfield, T. Wood, T. Privett and E.J. Baker. Financially, the Council had been able to hold down and even reduce the rates, despite the drain on their capital due to new mains water and sewage services, and expenditure on a considerable amount of tar paving throughout the town. What had assisted in their endeavours was the rise in the population – showing that the district was becoming more favoured as a residential area. In the Edwardian period, Petersfield's population rose from 3,267 to 3,947.

Under its next Chairman and Vice Chairman, Mr Cross and Mr Burley, however, the town's business was not going to be conducted so smoothly; from 1903 onwards, the market question became the subject of many heated debates and personal attacks. Indeed, such was the furore caused in the press by the warring factions on the Council that the Headmaster of Churcher's College, the Rev. W. Henry Bond, declared that "the townsmen of Petersfield are tired of "scenes" in the Urban Council." He called for the creation of four vacancies at the April 1907 elections; subsequently, four new men did stand for office: Messrs Seward, Bailey and Woods were elected, and Messrs Blair, Lines and Palmer were defeated: this seemed to solve the personal problems on the council. One beneficial result of the shenanigans in the Council was that the turnout at UDC election time was remarkably high: in 1906, for example, 582 electors cast their vote out of a total of 700 people entitled to vote; in 1907, this figure rose to 604. At the same time, the high turnout indicated a desire to cast a vote on the market question, but Messrs Blair and Lines, who were determined at all costs to keep the market in the Square, in fact lost their places on the Council in favour of more long-standing representatives, some of whom were of the same opinion on retaining the market. The electorate, perhaps not unexpectedly, had expressed their conservatism in their choice of representatives.

The outspoken views of Councillor J.P. Blair ("the working-men's candidate") – who once called the (former) workhouse "a Bastille" – frequently upset his colleagues. Despite – or maybe because of this – he collected a good number of votes at election time and had remained on the Board of Guardians for several years. He continued, too, to call a spade a spade at UDC meetings and was voted in at the 1904 elections, along with Dr. Leachman and Mr W.T. Neighbour. Blair won more support among "pro-marketeers" (councillors supporting its retention in the Square) the following year with the election of Messrs Privett and Sample to the Council. It was Councillor Blair who proposed, in 1906, that new Council Offices be built in Heath Road, adjacent to the Working Men's Club building. The council did use a building on that site at the time, but it was inadequate in size, poorly heated and dirty. Mr Blair was eventually obliged to resign from some of his municipal duties through ill health in 1910.

Deaths

Many personalities who had dominated the local political scene for decades passed away in the Edwardian decade. Of these, the death of John Bonham-Carter (the third of that name) at Christmastide in 1905 aroused the most distress within the immediate community and well beyond. The *Hants and Sussex News* summarised the occurrence thus:

> "No more startling, and in its immediate effect upon the community, no more paralysing an announcement has probably ever suddenly plunged the whole district into mourning, than the dreadful tidings which last Thursday morning were brought to the town from Adhurst that Mr Bonham-Carter had been found dead in the woods, not far from his mansion, with a wound in the forehead and a recently discharged revolver at his feet".

Bonham-Carter's suicide was partly attributed to his wife's grave state of health which, in turn, had had a depressing and debilitating effect on him. He had also twice suffered head injuries as a result of falls from his horse in recent years. He had relinquished the bulk of his public work and interests and devoted himself to his sick wife for many months. Bonham-Carter had given over twenty years of his life to the local community in various capacities and his loss was therefore particularly painful to bear under the circumstances. Fourteen years previously, he had married an American lady, had one son who had died in infancy and one daughter, currently aged nine. He was 52 years of age.

Grief at the death of John Bonham-Carter was compounded, a mere two weeks later, by the passing away of his wife, Mary Withers Bonham-Carter. For some time, her health had been deteriorating and, being incurable, it was no surprise to learn that she had succumbed to the disease. Like her husband, she had played a role in the community, both in Sheet and Petersfield. The following June, Mary Bonham-Carter's mother-in-law, Mary Baring Bonham-Carter, also died. She was the second wife and widow of John Bonham-Carter, her husband's father who had been the MP for Winchester from 1847 to 1874. She lived mostly in London and was in her 80th year.

The sudden and unexpected departure of this landowning family in the neighbourhood hastened the sale of their properties in the Edwardian period: his freehold estates in East Meon and Petersfield, which included much building land his shares in various businesses and the Rushes Common Estate were all put under the hammer at the Dolphin Hotel in June 1906. However, the sale of Rushes Common was called into question as it was claimed that it had not in fact formed part of the Bonham-Carter estate. Despite this, it was recommended that the UDC purchase the Common as common land for public use.

Local politics lost another familiar name towards the end of the Edwardian era when Mr William Nicholson, "the Squire of Basing Park", died at his London residence in 1909. He was born in 1824 into the famous 18th century London distillery firm of gin makers, J & W Nicholson and Company, which lent the money to the Marylebone Cricket Club to buy the freehold to Lord's Cricket Ground in the mid-nineteenth century. The MCC subsequently adopted the Nicholson Company's colours of red and gold as their own. When he first moved to Basing Park, he took a leading part in public affairs in the district; when Sir William Jolliffe was elevated to the peerage in 1866, Nicholson was invited to become the Liberal candidate for the Borough and he was elected unopposed and remained as Petersfield's M.P. until he was beaten by the Conservative, the Hon. Sydney Hylton Jolliffe – by a mere 16 votes – in 1874. However, he regained his seat in 1880 and held it until 1885, when, under the Redistribution Act of that year, Petersfield was merged into the constituency of East Hampshire. Ironically, it was his son, Mr W.G. Nicholson, standing as a Conservative, who was returned as the local M.P. in 1897.

William Nicholson, who became a Deputy Lieutenant for Hampshire, was most generous towards religious, educational and social agencies: he entirely funded the building of Privett Church, paid a good proportion of the restoration costs of St. Peter's Church in Petersfield in the 1870s, financially supported Churcher's College and gave the school its land on Ramshill, and, as one of the largest landowners in the county, served as a practical agriculturalist on his estates.

With the death in 1907 of John Gammon, whose home was at Herne House, Petersfield lost a large employer of labour and one of the chief property owners of the town who had helped to shape the town itself. His father had been a carpenter and builder in Petersfield and, with his brother Andrew, the firm of J. and A. Gammon thrived for many years, then became J. Gammon and Son when his son, T.G. Gammon, joined them. They became the chief building firm in the district until 1904, when they were taken over by their rivals, Messrs J. Holder and Son (although John Holder had married Miss Gammon). John Gammon was responsible for building properties in Tilmore Terrace, Madeline Road and Penns Road (all built on land purchased from the railway company after the Midhurst line was constructed); most of Charles Street, the row of shops in Chapel Street, and the villa residences overlooking the Heath. To his building operations, he added farming and hop-growing. He had purchased Herne House and farm in the 1870s, then farms at Bolinge Hill, Buriton and Langrish. He further developed into brickmaking and ran brickworks in Steep Marsh, Liss and Stroud.

His public career involved being a member of the Highway Board, the School Board and Rural Sanitary Authority and he was also a Guardian of the Poor, served on the Gas Board, the Corn Exchange Company and as a trustee of the Congregational Church, which his firm built in the 1880s as well as the Salvation Army hall in Swan Street.

The town had lost another member of an old family in the town in 1903: William Mould had been one of the few surviving links with Petersfield from the early Victorian days. He died at the then remarkable age of 86. He was best known as the lessee of the market, but had also been a farmer, corn merchant and dairyman, living at Buckmore Farm and carrying on his building and funeral business in Chapel Street for 60 years. In 1900, he moved this business to Dragon Street, at the corner of St. Peter's Road, and used the outbuildings there as a carpenter's and monumental mason's shop.

CHAPTER 5

The Death of Edward VII

The Edwardian era came to an end in May 1910 with the sudden death of the King from bronchitis, aggravated by several heart attacks. The King died just before midnight on a Friday, but, although the Post Office had had an intimation of it very early the next morning, the publication of the news only reached Petersfield when the *Portsmouth Evening News* arrived in the town with the milk train at about 7 a.m. The London papers arrived soon afterwards and were much in demand.

Queen Victoria's burial day had been conducted in depressing weather conditions; King Edward's was met with brilliant spring sunshine. Petersfield paid its own tribute with a grand procession through the town involving several hundred participants marking the end of a notable decade.

The day of the King's funeral was marked with amnity: shops, banks and public houses were closed all day; the railway station was shut for several hours as very few trains were running; a large one-hour long procession wound its way round the town and Square to St. Peter's for a memorial service.

Memorial procession around the Square for King Edward, 1910

Older people still remembered the many previous occasions when a monarch's health had failed: in December 1861, at the death of Prince Albert, when Queen Victoria had been inconsolable; in the winter of 1871, when this Edward (then Prince of Wales) had contracted typhoid and had hovered between life and death; in January 1901, when the nation lost their Queen of 63 years; and the following June, when all the preparations for the King's coronation were made and the news came that his life was again in danger.

As a diplomatist during WWI, and an architect of the "entente cordiale" with France, Edward VII was remembered as "The Peacemaker". There was "an intense feeling of grief and pain" in Petersfield, according the *Hants & Sussex News*, whose next three issues were bordered with black. Characteristic of the sentiments expressed was the "demonstration of sympathy and sorrow so manifestly real, and the tribute paid to their late sovereign so genuinely loyal and affectionate" that Petersfield "bore its part with a quiet dignity and a unity of feeling that did the community credit."

In 1905, the *Hants and Sussex News* had carried a brief article about a Mrs Charlotte

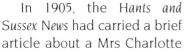

Memorial procession around the Square for King Edward, 1910

Carter, who had the distinction of being a subject under five monarchs: currently resident at the Temperance Hotel in the Square, she recounted how she had been born towards the end of George III's reign (when she was named Charlotte after the then Queen). Despite her advanced years (close to 90 years of age), she still possessed an almost inexhaustible energy and an indomitably strong will, which was the secret of her staying power. In her spare time, she made rugs, was happy to ride in a trailer towed behind a bicycle and declared that she hoped one day to achieve her ambition of riding in "a fast-going motor car".

CHAPTER 6

Edwardian Steep

T he beech and yew-covered hangers enveloping Steep and Froxfield, whose beauty had been immortalised by William Cobbett and Gilbert White, became the focus of interest of practitioners of the Arts and Crafts Movement during the Edwardian era. Steep village found itself heavily influenced by this remarkable artistic, social and architectural revolution. The local architectural practice of Unsworth, Son & Triggs had a large hand in this, but the principal factor was the presence of, and influence exerted by, Bedales School at the heart of the village.

Just seven years after Bedales had been founded by John Haden Badley near Haywards Heath in Sussex, this pioneering, independent and co-educational boarding school arrived in Steep in 1900, when Badley purchased the old Steephurst Farm and 100 acres of farmland. Although the new main Bedales building was designed by E.P. Warren, who had been recommended to Badley by the owner of the original school in Sussex, Badley left the designs for further developments to local architects (like W.F. Unsworth) or accepted the

W.F. Unsworth's office in Petersfield

recommendation of others (such as Ernest Gimson), both of whom had been strongly influenced by the Arts and Crafts movement. There were to be many strong links between the re-foundation of Bedales School in Steep and the work of the creative designers and architects of the new movement, viz:

In 1901, the Head Boy of Bedales, Geoffrey Lupton, whose family came from an engineering background, left the school to become an apprentice cabinet-maker under a key member of the original Arts and Crafts movement, Ernest Gimson. Lupton built his own house and workshop in Cockshott Lane in the neighbouring village of Froxfield in 1908.

In 1905, the purchase of Restalls in Church Road, Steep, by Unsworth (senior) ensured that an Arts and Crafts influence was implanted in Steep in the Edwardian era. The successful Petersfield partnership of the Unsworths, father and son, and the garden designer and English country house architect, Harry Inigo Triggs, whose office was situated in Station Road, Petersfield, continued to have an influence on the town for many years. It was Triggs who was responsible for the restoration of the statue of William III in the Square in 1913 and who designed the town's War Memorial in 1922.

Restalls in Steep

In 1910, Edward Barnsley, born into a family of furniture makers, was sent to Bedales by his father Ernest because the school encouraged the learning of practical skills and craftwork. He, too, settled in nearby Froxfield.

In 1911, the poet, Edward Thomas, arrived in Steep with his wife Helen so that they could send their children to Bedales Prep. School, Dunhurst. Edward Thomas's wife Helen taught at the school for a while and the Thomas family soon became friends with Geoffrey Lupton.

Other connections and coincidences abound: in the late 1880s, a young medical student, Harry Roberts, had attended lectures by William Morris at Kelmscott House (Morris's London home) for the Socialist League; in 1908, Harry bought 34 acres of land at Oakshott Hanger and built himself a weekend retreat from his Stepney practice, using it first as a sanatorium for his tuberculosis patients, but later turning it into a convivial meeting place for many artists and intellectuals. It was Geoffrey Lupton who introduced Edward Thomas to Harry Roberts when the latter first arrived at Oakshott but, sadly, the two had only a brief acquaintanceship, as Thomas was killed at Arras in 1917; in the 1920s, Harry Roberts' son-in-law, George Marston, began work at the newly established Rural Industries Bureau, a body supporting country trades and handicrafts; finally, Eric Gill, the sculptor, wood engraver and Fabian Socialist, who had settled in Ditchling in 1907, designed the logo for the Petersfield Musical Festival in 1935 to coincide with the Festival's move to the newly-completed Town Hall in Heath Road, the funds for which had been raised by Harry Roberts.

We can draw a parallel between the aims of the Arts and Crafts movement and those of the new Bedales under Badley: while the Arts and Crafts practitioners sought to re-establish the harmony between architect, designer and craftsman which had been devalued as a result of the Industrial Revolution, the new educational opportunities of Bedales represented an alternative response to the rigid educational systems prevailing in independent schools of the time. Both movements therefore contained elements of revolutionary social thinking; both saw themselves as part of a wider arena of social reform and working conditions; both had come to the conclusion that the ideal – and idyllic – setting for the development of their ethos

Bedales Library

was the rural, even rustic, simple life where art and education were promoted as a way of life. They even shared a common motto: "Head, Hand and Heart", first used by the Society of Designers in 1896 ('Head' for creativity and imagination, 'Hand' for skill and craft, 'Heart' for honesty and for love). So the products of the craftsmen and the educationalists coincided in all these respects.

William Whiteman, in his book on *The Edward Thomas Country*, says of Bedales: "In greater or lesser degree, Bedales had all the ingredients [of the extremes of a progressive movement] – co-education, the simple life, disciplinary rigours, the open air, hygiene, Ruskin and Morris, Arts and Crafts, Liberty dresses, folk dancing, vegetarianism, teetotalism, pacifism, intellectual liberalism, pink middle-class socialism, votes for women, moral earnestness."

It was William Morris who had first insisted on the integration of buildings and their gardens, thereby encouraging a new movement in English garden design. Later, thanks to the contemporary popularity of gardens among the Edwardian middle classes, this integration became part and parcel of the work of the Arts and Crafts designers such as Inigo Triggs and W.F. Unsworth. It was Triggs who was the link between the Arts and Crafts houses within Steep: he designed Unsworth's garden at Restalls, where the characteristic Arts and Crafts mix of formal design and abundant flower beds, of split level gardens, water features, brick paths, yew hedging and topiary, shrubbery and balustraded terraces all feature.

Harry Inigo Triggs

The Edwardian period, then, had been a remarkable one by any standards for the small community of Steep. As if the combined legacy of such luminaries as Unsworth, Triggs, Thomas, Roberts, Lupton, Badley, and Barnsley were not sufficient to make it a remarkable village, other notable residents have been the poet and artist Thomas Sturge Moore, an almost exact contemporary of Harry Roberts, and the novelist John Wyndham, an old Bedalian of the inter-war years.

CHAPTER 7

1911-1914

Introduction

The census year 1911 revealed that the population of England and Wales had risen to 32.5 million; the population of Petersfield stood at 3,947, a rise of approximately 20% over the previous decade.

The long, hot summer of 1911 – which had stretched from early May until mid-September – ushered in the House of Windsor, when 1% of the population owned 70% of the country's wealth, a docker was paid sixpence an hour and East Enders slept five to a bed, Rupert Brooke was describing the heart of England as a dreamy Arcadia, "perpetually June and always six o'clock of a warm afternoon", in short, a benign (social) dictatorship.

The new reign was ushered in by a new-look *Hants & Sussex News*, with a front page including one central article among the usual advertisements – often for stabling at various hotels and inns – and the back page dedicated to sports news and results. Page 3 ran articles entitled "Garden Gossip" and "Home Hints". In the body of the paper, there appeared for the first time a large advert accompanied by a photo; it was for the Lavant Street grocer's W.J. Fuller [now Petersfield Photographic] and it began a trend towards more illustrated adverts – frequently for food or clothes shops – and even some news items backed up with photographs.

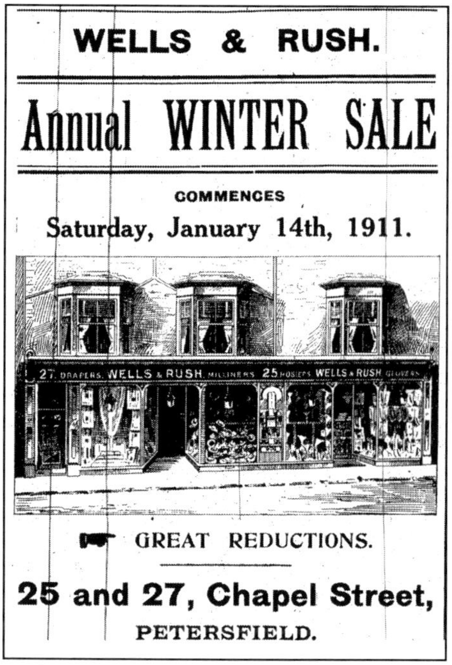

WELLS & RUSH.

Annual WINTER SALE

COMMENCES

Saturday, January 14th, 1911.

☞ GREAT REDUCTIONS.

25 and 27, Chapel Street,

PETERSFIELD.

The Wells and Rush Winter Sale, 1911

The Coronation of George V

Whether by chance or design, the Programme of Festivities in Petersfield for the Coronation of George V in June 1911 coincided with the second notice of sale of the estates of the Right Hon. Lord Hylton. With the cynicism of hindsight, we can wonder which of these two events attracted the greater interest – or enthusiasm!

The town's programme of celebrations began with a peal of bells at St. Peter's at 6 a.m. It was followed at the more convenient time of 11 o'clock with a service in the church and, three-quarters of an hour later, its continuation in the Square. Thereafter, a "Dinner to the Old People" was held in the Drill Hall and decorated vehicles paraded through the town, followed by a further peal of bells.

A carnival procession around the town took place in the afternoon, headed by the Victoria Brass Band, and schoolchildren marched from their schools to the Square to be met by various societies and

The notice of the celebration in Petersfield for the Coronation of George V

the Fire Brigade to sing God save the King and Salute the Flag on the church tower. The rest of the afternoon was given over to sports on the Heath, a children's tea, an adults' tea (two sittings) and finishing with the distribution of Coronation Mugs to children at 7 p.m.

Petersfield Square at the 1911 Coronation

Sadly, rain and wind marred the festivities and played havoc with the decorations people had displayed for the day; no outdoor illuminations were possible for two days, but, in the evenings of that week, the Misses Pickering's studios in Lavant Street displayed an exhibition of lantern pictures taken on Coronation Day itself in the town. To complete the week's events, a Coronation Ball was held in the Drill Hall, organised by the Petersfield Territorials.

Sale of the Hylton Estate

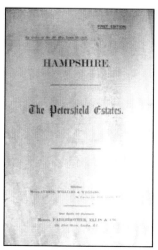

The Hylton Estates Sale notice, 1911

Preliminary details of this sale first appeared in the press in April 1911, giving a list of the "compact farms, smallholdings, nurseries, accommodation and building land" available, totalling about 335 acres. In the centre of the town, there were shops and houses and numerous cottages and gardens for sale by auction. With the Manor of Petersfield itself, the income value of the long-leasehold and "fee farm" rents was estimated at around £2,000 per annum. The whole offer formed "sound investments for trustees and capitalists" and "an excellent opportunity for builders and others desirous of securing sites for the erection of residences and villas and also for the tenants of acquiring the freehold of their holdings".

Further information showed more precise details of the properties for sale and their income value to potential owners; there were 30 farms (including Tilmore, Little Tilmore, Heath and Causeway farms); 26 town properties (situated in the Square, High Street, Dragon Street, College Street, Hylton Road, Heath Road, St. Peter's Road and Sussex Road); 64 cottages (both detached and semi-detached properties, and some in blocks); and a total of £126 per annum income from grounds rents and leases from public buildings, shops and first-class residences.

The Auction Sale was advertised for July; this took place at the Dolphin Hotel in the High Street and the auction items were divided into 104 lots, which took just four hours to complete. About 20 items were left unsold, and the total amount realised was over £22,000. Lord Hylton's estates had been in the (erstwhile Jolliffe) family for over 200 years, but circumstances had led him to dispose of them through the firm of Messrs Fairbrother, Ellis and Co.

The auctioneer prefaced his remarks to the public present with the statement that he could not help thinking that the future of Petersfield depended to a very large extent on the dispersal of this property; Lord Hylton had instructed him to keep the reserve prices low and that, as soon as these were reached, this should be disclosed to the room because the next day the reserve prices might be raised. Lord Hylton clearly had in mind that his tenants should become owners and that, since times were changing rapidly, this was a perfect opportunity for individuals to purchase properties for themselves.

The land on the whole sold at very reasonable prices, but the sale of the farms caused some hesitation, with the land around Heath House (in Sussex Road) producing only one bid for the 64 acres of pasture. It was bought by Mr J.R. Bennion. Causeway and Tilmore Farms were not sold at the auction.

Heath House

Three lots aroused the interest of the public; first, lot 9: "The Manor or reputed Manor of Petersfield, with its lands, rights, privileges and appurtenances, including the portion of the Heath Pond lying in the said Manor". The auctioneer said he hoped that someone that day would become lord of the manor – "it was not every day that one could buy

a manor" – but, with no bids near the suggested price, the lot was passed over. Second, lot 34: the Petersfield Working Men's Institute; this went to Mr Schwerdt of Old Alresford House, who in fact let it to the Liberal Club, but re-sold it the following November. Third, lot 67 was the statue of King William III, on which the auctioneer put a small reserve figure, because he felt sure someone would want to leave it there for the benefit of the town and that, out of a public-spiritedness, the Town ought

The (former) Working Men's Institute in Heath Road

to pay for it. This was precisely what happened, when Mr Percy C. Burley, the Clerk to the UDC, bought it on their behalf for £120.

Certain lots in the auction were purchased by the UDC for the benefit of the town, notably lot 2: 22 acres of common land for the purposes of establishing a domestic refuse tip for all time (such waste had until then been dumped on Butser Hill); lot 67: the hurdle house and the freehold land between there and the entrance to the church; the soil of the Square and the statue of William III; lot 8: 18 acres of freehold land on the Heath known locally as the Horse Piece (to prevent construction on this area which could be given over to a recreation ground and an 18 hole golf course).

The Butser Cutting in Victorian times

Lot 53 in the Sale was the corner plot at the junction of the Spain and Swan Street; this had been a timber and corrugated motor shed and workshops and stables which was leased by Mr Ewan, a local engineer and building contractor, who bought the premises and transformed them into the Forge as we still know it today. Part of the building housed an extraordinary vehicle which was used as a sand lorry during the week and at weekends converted into a charabanc with removable seats, the first such vehicle in the district.

The sudden death occurred, in January 1912, of Captain the Hon. William Sydney Hylton Jolliffe, the only surviving son of the first Lord Hylton (formerly Sir William Jolliffe, Bart.), which occasioned the sale of his home, Heath House, in Sussex Road. Coming barely six months after the sale of the Hylton Estate, this death hastened the complete demise of the Jolliffe family in Petersfield, where they had first settled after John Jolliffe, inheriting his wife's Petersfield estate on her death in 1731, had bought the manorial rights to the borough from Edward Gibbon (father of the historian) in 1739. Numerous memorial tablets to the various members of the family may still be seen in St. Peter's Church, although the cemetery containing most of the family's graves is to be found in Merstham, near Redhill, in Surrey.

Captain Jolliffe had taken up residence in Heath House in 1870 and, like his father, grandfather and great-grandfather before him, became the Borough's M.P. in 1874. More recently, he had held many offices, such as Chairman of the Petersfield Conservative Association and, as a J.P., Chairman of the Magistrates for Petersfield Petty Sessions. Described as "an aristocrat to his fingertips", he habitually discharged his civic duties with courtesy and charm. He had also once attempted – unsuccessfully – to rescue three schoolboys who had fallen through the ice on the Heath Pond.

The manorial rights to the Heath were finally purchased in 1914 by the UDC from its joint owners, Lord Hylton and Mr Lothian Bonham-Carter, but not before a further year's debate had taken place. This was made possible by the agreement for a loan to the UDC by the Local Government Board and brought to a close the question of the town owning the Heath and Pond for Petersfield's residents after more than ten years of wrangling.

The restoration of the statue of William III

It had already been noted in a letter from Petersfield historian E. Arden Minty to the *Hants and Sussex News* in 1910 that the statue in the Square was "falling to pieces" and that, although the repair of a lead statue was not a simple matter, he said "it would be a disgrace to the town if we allowed it to perish." The baton in William's hand had already been broken off when a string of flags was tied to it during the Diamond Jubilee celebrations for Queen Victoria in 1897.

William III before restoration

Harry Inigo Triggs, the Arts and Crafts architect (of Messrs. Unsworth, Son and Triggs), had also complained that to leave a fine, leaden statue to remain in its present condition was a disgrace to the town. He left no doubt as to its artistic merit, calling it almost unique among England's, or indeed Europe's, existing portrait statues in lead. It was in no way inferior to its replicas and it was comparable as an equestrian statue to those of St. Mark's, Venice. In Petersfield's example, the unfortunate practice of painting it periodically had allowed nearly all traces of the fine surface ornament of the robes and the delicate modelling of both the horse and rider to disappear. The action of the sun, too, had caused the statue to lean considerably. Inigo Triggs called upon the Council to raise the necessary funds to undertake the work, to which he would be pleased to contribute. The town surveyor, Mr Keates, had examined the statue and confirmed that there was a great thickness of paint on it, that one leg of the horse had been unwisely repaired by filling it with plaster of Paris, and that it was being supported by a rod filled with plaster. Consequently, Mr Triggs was approached by the Council for his report and recommendations on the statue's restoration.

Mr Triggs made his report in conjunction with a Mr Laidler of Fulham. In it, the statue was described as a fine example of early 18th century leadwork, probably one of only half a dozen such equestrian statues in the country. It required action to remedy the effects of both sun and frost, which had caused cracks and fissures in its body and legs. With the help of a sturdy scaffold, the horse could be supported to allow straightening and strengthening to take place. Layers of paint should be removed, the baton replaced with one identical to those on the similar statues in Bristol or Edinburgh, the whole statue should be re-gilt as formerly and the protective railings around the statue should be removed, with the lower step enlarged to resemble a pedestal. The whole cost of the restoration would amount to £133.

A letter in the press from "Petersfieldiensis" in September 1911 made the point that William's "baton" was not originally intended as a military symbol, but was a scroll representing the Declaration of Rights which William was compelled to accept when the crown was offered to him.

With added support from Professor W. Robert Colton, Professor of Sculpture to the Royal Academy and other reputed judges, an appeal for funds – amounting to £350 – to pay for the restoration was made that December and, to encourage a good civic response, there was a call on the pride and the public spirit of Petersfielders to rise to the occasion to save this work of art which "conferred a distinction on the town of which many a larger town might be proud".

In the climate of the Glorious Revolution of 1688 which brought the Protestant William III to the throne, it was Bristol which first sought to prove its loyalty to the Crown (via the House of Orange) by erecting a statue to the King in Queen's Square; not to be outdone, Hull followed Bristol's example and put up a statue in 1734, which still stands in their Market Place. In 1750, Petersfield's MP, Sir William Jolliffe, left £500 in his will for the purchase of the statue we still have today. His support for a monarch whom he considered "our great deliverer from Popery, Slavery and Arbitrary Power" had brought him personal wealth and prestige as well as lucrative positions in the City of London.

William is depicted as Marcus Aurelius and the work is attributed to John Cheere, probably working in conjunction with his brother Henry (later, Sir Henry Cheere); the statue was erected in the circus in front of the Jolliffes' Petersfield House in New Way [now St. Peter's Road] in 1757, but removed to the Square in 1812 after the House was demolished in 1793.

A comment on the bow on the tail of William's horse by Moutray Head in his *Highways and Byways in Hampshire* in 1909 had even elicited an amusing poem from a reader of the *Hants and Sussex News*:

By early 1913, estimates had been obtained and the work started on William by the firm of Singer and Sons of Frome (who cast the statue of King Alfred in Winchester); a copper plate was found inside the body of the horse recording the fact that it had been "repaired and new iron'd" in June 1825 by R. Young. Unfortunately, Young had filled up some of the inside with cement and this appeared to have been the cause of its subsequent decay.

Oh, Highways, Byways,
  I wonder how you dare
Make comments disrespectful
  On our Statue in the Square.

It's only but twelve months ago,
  We were mostly unaware,
There was artistic merit,
  In our Statue in the Square.

But since we've been instructed,
  We one and all declare,
We have a damaged " chef d'œuvre,
  In our Statue in the Square.

Then Highways, Byways,
  It's enough to make one swear,
When you dub " fat beast" the noble steed,
  Who prances in the Square.

You say he's a ponderous prancer,
  I think it is rude of you,
Though he's pranced so long all on one side,
  He has to be propped, it is true.

Then the bow on the horse's tail,
  You think is a matter of fun,
You forget it is meant for a " beau ideal,"
  Round the tail of the horse that is spun.

But wait a while, and you will see
  The drab with gold will glare,
And more sturdily will prance the horse
  On his platform in the Square.

Then Highways, Byways,
  When you've an hour to spare,
Pray come again and visit
  Our Statue in the Square.
                              Low-Ways.

Poem to William III's statue for visitors

However, after almost six months' work and a final donation of £22 from the Loyal Orange Institution, the publicly-subscribed newly-restored statue was unveiled by Lord Selborne in a grand manner on 3rd September 1913. The iron railings had been removed and a granite step put in their place and the Latin inscription was corrected and renewed on the pedestal. A special bottle obtained from Timothy White's in Chapel Street [now the Job Centre], containing a history of the statue and a record of the work carried out, was sealed and deposited inside the horse. At the official opening ceremony, the Petersfield Company and Band of the 6th Hants Regiment in their scarlet uniforms marched from the Drill Hall to the station, where they were met by about 40 Orangemen from Portsmouth, then on to the Square where the National Reserve and the Petersfield Fire Brigade were on parade. Speeches by W.C. Burley for the UDC, Miss Marjorie Bowen, an authority of the life of William III, and the Earl of Selborne himself completed the afternoon's ceremony. At that week's meeting of the UDC, a letter was read out which had been addressed to the Queen of the Netherlands, informing her that there were in Britain five equestrian statues of King William: in

The unveiling ceremony, 1913

London, Dublin, Bristol and Hull, "and in the market place of the little town of Petersfield in Hampshire". Queen Wilhelmina (who had come to the throne at the age of 10 in 1890 and was to reign for 58 years) graciously gave Petersfield the honour of her patronage to the ceremony.

The restored statue

William was now restored: one side of the statue had to be raised by over a foot as it had sunk away from the perpendicular; all four legs had to be remodelled, the hind legs having almost entirely perished; the internal structure was also remodelled and the weight of the rider supported by a steel bar; the reins were renewed; and the scroll was replaced in the King's right hand. The harness, accoutrements and the wreath on the King's head were gilded, lending a most pleasing and contrasting effect against the grey of the lead.

The demolition of Castle House

This fine building, described in the *Victoria County History of Hampshire* in 1908 as "architecturally the most interesting domestic building in the town", dated from the early years of the 17th century, but retained the mediaeval arrangement of a central block with wings at right angles to it at either end. The entrance lobby recalled a mediaeval central hall, but the chief living rooms were on the ground and first floor in

The Square with Castle House

the north wing. Much of its original panelling and several fine chimney pieces were still preserved and it had kept its kitchen yard on the north side and a long garden stretching to the west. The front façade was obscured by ivy, but imposing wrought-iron railings and a gateway leading to a small forecourt lent it grandeur.

E. Arden Minty repeats the proposition that there was once a religious house on this site, with the corroboration that, in Victorian times, a tunnel which led to St. Peter's church had been discovered under its foundations.

The house purportedly contained carving by Grinling Gibbons (who had also worked at Petworth House). Unfortunately, there is no accurate record of the building's construction date, nor of its first owners (except their initials E.M. and W.M., which were carved above the front door), but one well-known local family, the Bilsons, did purchase the house in the middle of the 17th century. Thereafter, as we have seen, the house passed to the Jolliffes, then the Bonhams and the Bonham-Carters until the mid-nineteenth century; it then became a school from the 1860s to its closure in 1895. The building reverted to private ownership and was occupied first by the Lord Bishop of Southampton, the Right Rev. The Hon. Arthur Temple Lyttleton and his wife, then by the Rev. E.M. Tomlinson, a retired vicar from East Meon, until 1908. It was offered for sale by public auction in 1912 but, despite a plea in the press by Mr Fleet Goldsmith that July for the UDC to seize the "exceptional opportunity" to purchase the House and use it for offices, it was put up for sale by auction at the Dolphin Hotel. Few people attended the event but bidding stopped at £2,300, when the auctioneer announced that the Court of Chancery would not allow him to sell at that figure. However, the plot and building did eventually go to a private buyer, a certain Mr Rye, and the whole site started to be sold off piecemeal. First, a strip of land on the Chapel Street side of the property was advertised for sale for the purpose of road widening. In February 1913, the owner's solicitors, Shield and Mackarness [now Mackarness and Lunt], advertised this plot for £600, which necessitated the pulling down of the north wing of Castle House, the work to be carried out "at once". In May that year, the auctioneers Hall, Pain and Goldsmith received instructions to sell five 60 ft. freehold building plots in the garden of Castle House which extended along Swan Street.

The most interesting development in the Castle House saga occurred in July 1913, when it was reported at a UDC meeting that the great Scottish-American industrialist and philanthropist, Mr Andrew Carnegie, had, through his secretary, practically invited the UDC to save Castle House by buying it in order to turn it into a library – at his expense – for Petersfield. (It had recently been reported in *The Times* that the Carnegie Institution had handed £2m. to trustees for the establishment of public libraries, schools and universities throughout the United States and the UK). However, the UDC again rejected the proposal, saying that all the library accommodation that could be filled on a 1d. rate would not account for more than 2 rooms out of a total of 43 and the most which could be charged

Andrew Carnegie in 1913

to the library account was 5%. The Carnegie Institution replied that if the UDC wished to procure library buildings, it was up to them to levy the 1d. rate. The council decided that, under the circumstances, they could not pursue the scheme any further.

Castle House was demolished in January 1914 to the sound of the wailing and gnashing of teeth by Petersfield residents and by a flow of crocodile tears from Urban District Councillors. The measured and delicately-phrased

Castle House

account in the *Hants and Sussex News* of January 7th hid the outright hypocrisy and justifiable fury behind the headlines:

> The Urban Council seriously considered the practicability of trying to get possession of [Castle House] on behalf of the town, but decided that they would not be warranted in venturing on the necessary expenditure. Whether they were wise in their conclusion is a point upon which there is some difference of opinion amongst the townsfolk but, at anyrate, the chance of acquiring the place was let slip with the almost inevitable result that the disappearance of this historic old dwelling was shortly bound to ensue.

Tragically, the press report concludes with the words: *There will always remain the reflection that Petersfield was lacking in public spirit to allow such a relic of the past to disappear altogether from the scene.* The infamous Mr Rye now pursued his demand for £600 for the strip of land on the north side of the House to enable the council to widen the High Street at that point. The council again demurred and offered a maximum of £250. The resulting stand-off lasted for many years, with the old Castle House site remaining an empty space of memories until 1922, when the present buildings were constructed.

Stanley Johnson, whose father was one of the councillors at the time of the Castle House fiasco, recalled that "the UDC was mean in not buying Castle House. It could have bought it instead of allowing it to be pulled down". As a young man himself at the time (he was born in 1888), his memories were of a Council which was particularly averse to spending money on property for the benefit of the town. Lyndum House, for example, which had earlier been offered for sale at £800, had also been rejected.

But 1914 was by no means the last time that the Council was to be held to ransom by a developer.

The Suffragette Movement

Bedales had again played host to a fête and meeting in support of Woman's Suffrage in the summer of 1911. The speaker, the ardent suffragist Miss Evelyn Sharp, felt that this venue was particularly apt for such a meeting, as it was already fulfilling the criteria for equal chances being given to both boys and girls. Indeed, when their battle was fought and won, they could say that it had been partly won on the playing fields of Bedales!

Evelyn Sharp selling Votes for Women, *1909*

But, the following year, 1912, was a turning point for the suffragettes in the UK – more particularly in London – as they turned to using more militant tactics, such as chaining themselves to railings, setting fire to the contents of letterboxes, smashing windows and occasionally detonating bombs. This was because the current Prime Minister, H. H. Asquith, was on the point of giving women (over 30 and either married to a property-owner or owning a property themselves) the right to vote, but he made a volte-face at the last minute, as he thought that women might vote against him in the next General Election and prevent his Liberal party from coming to power.

Another meeting at Bedales in March addressed the question of the suffragettes' new militancy: Mrs Badley believed that it was impossible to explain what made one person militant and another non-militant, but she argued that both constitutional and militant methods were valid and necessary in the struggle to bring women the vote and that both acted in the interests of the Woman's Suffrage Movement. Even after the militant outrages that March, the most recent of three Conciliation Bills which had passed through parliament in 1910,1911 and 1912, all of which aimed to give at least some women the vote, had been defeated by a mere 14 votes.

In December, it was announced that the Petersfield M.P., Mr W.G. Nicholson, had promised to receive a deputation from the local Woman's Suffrage Society by the end of the year and that Lady Selborne would be among their number. The Petersfield group had recently combined with 16 other such groups to form an alliance. The deputation numbered about 30 altogether, from several societies in the constituency and both political parties. However, Mr Nicholson declined to be bound to one particular course of action; he reserved for himself the right to oppose the Bill or not. But he did add the comment that he was in favour of limited suffrage for women.

The Petersfield Woman's Suffrage Society was by now increasing its membership and between 300 and 400 people attended their next fête at Bedales in 1913. This was the year that one suffragette, Emily Davison, died after throwing herself under the King's horse at the Epsom Derby in June. Many of her fellow suffragettes were imprisoned and went on a hunger strike as a scare tactic against the government.

During World War I there was a serious shortage of able-bodied men, and women were required to take on many of the traditional male roles — this led to a new view of what a woman was capable of doing. The war also caused a split in the British Suffragette Movement, with the mainstream, represented by Emmeline and Christabel Pankhurst calling a 'ceasefire' in their campaign for the duration of the war, while more radical suffragettes, represented by Sylvia Pankhurst's Women's Suffrage Federation continued the struggle. The National Union of Women's Suffrage Societies, which had always employed "constitutional" methods, continued to lobby during the war years and compromises were worked out with the coalition government. The Representation of the People Act was passed in 1918, enfranchising women over the age of 30 who met minimum property qualifications. In November 1918, the Eligibility of Women Act was passed, allowing women to be elected into Parliament. Finally, the Representation of the People Act 1928 extended the voting franchise to all women over the age of 21, granting women the vote on the same terms as men.

Emmeline Pankhurst

Leisure pursuits

Plans for Petersfield's first cinema – the Petersfield Electric Theatre – were published in the *Hants and Sussex News* in May 1911. A Petersfield architect, Mr W. Bates White, was hired to design the building, which was to replace the old Swan Inn on the same site at the corner of Chapel Street and Swan Street. It was a case of "no expense spared" for the audience

The Petersfield Electric Theatre

of 400, with new "tip-up" seating upholstered in plush, electric light inside the auditorium and, hopefully, all to be ready for the Coronation the next month. The opening had to be postponed until August, however, because of the "Great Railway Strike" that summer. The first showing of films included views of the Coronation procession and the Naval Review, which the audience applauded, followed by some "mirth-provoking developments" such as "The Animated Arm Chair", and "Charlie's Aunt" and, by way of contrast, some thrilling and dramatic situations such as "The Saw Mill Hero" and "Marozia", the latter representing a piece of 10th century Italian history in a series of coloured pictures. There was to be a change of programme every Monday and Thursday and two performances were held nightly.

The press report on the Heath Fair of 1911 reveals a good deal about the social mix of those attending, the types of problems encountered, but also the general fun associated with it:

The Taro Fair in Edwardian times

> The crowd attending the Fair was made up of all the usual elements, and represented every class and section of the inhabitants of the district for many miles around. The Fair is the recognised annual meeting-place of country people of the labouring class, and no doubt many had travelled long distances to be present. Many old habitués among the caravan folk and others who frequent the Fair for business purposes were recognised, and we were told that one patriarchal individual walked into the Fair for the 72nd successive year, while another, a well-known and familiar dealer in cutlery, celebrated his jubilee as an attendant at the Fair.

Present that year for the first time were the Red Cross, in charge of the Petersfield Women's and Men's V.A.D. (Voluntary Aid Detachments), while the police kept the usual order, pleased that the sale of "squirters" had been prohibited. There was still some profuse use of confetti, but, in general, the behaviour was not in any way riotous. The Fair was its usual mixture of business and entertainment: the Cattle Fair in the morning brought horses, sheep and horned stock for sale by auction, and the Pleasure Fair attracted hundreds to its fairground amusements. Occasional licences to sell alcohol at the Fair were granted to some public houses: in 1913, for example, the Bell Inn, the Volunteer Arms, the Old Drum and the Cricketers in Steep were given such licences.

The Heath was the focus for other kinds of entertainment: over the Whitsun weekend, there were sports such as cricket, bowls and quoits, and a fairground atmosphere was ensured by Fred Kimber's swingboats and coconut shies. Fire balloons were sent up and people danced to music by the Victoria Brass Band in the evening. After a precarious existence over a period of years, the first performance by the newly-constituted Petersfield Victoria Brass Band was held in July 1912 on Sheet Green in the afternoon and the Square in the evening. Bathing in the Heath Pond was permitted, even at certain points before 9 a.m. and after 7 p.m.; a canvas shelter was set up as a "dressing shed" in the sand pit at Music Hill and regulations regarding bathing dresses were in force. A Pierrot Troupe were also given permission to perform on the Heath for several evenings.

Bathing in the Heath Pond

In 1914, the five "Kaffir Singing Boys" returned to Petersfield for a second time to give concerts at the Congregational Church and the Corn Exchange, singing hymns in English and Kaffir; they represented the five tribes of the Basuto, Zulu, Red Kaffir, Fingo and Hottentot brought from Africa by Mr Balmer, a lecturer on African affairs, and Miss Elsie Clark, whose home was in Rhodesia.

Another exotic experience was that of the three-day Egyptian Bazaar held in the Corn Exchange in 1912, organised by the Wesleyans. The plain hall was transformed into a vivid and realistic scene from a Cairo street designed and constructed by Mr Alfred Stubley of Lincolnshire. Mosques and minarets, an obelisk and palms, coloured lanterns and flowers decorated the whole hall, which attracted hundreds, with the aim of raising funds for the Wesleyan church and its mission.

The town hosted its usual complement of circuses and menageries and a one-day performance by the Royal Italian Circus in the meadow by the Volunteer Arms brought elephants, Hungarian and Arabian horses, zebras, monkeys, bears, seals, and sea lions in September 1913.

The Petersfield Musical Festival continued to grow: in 1912, there was a total of over a hundred subscribers to the Festival, twenty-one competing choirs, and audience numbers showed that the event had become a permanent fixture in the town's calendar. Publicity for the Festival was helped by the annual profusion of photographs of the choirs appearing in the press. Dr. Hugh Allen, who brought with him a selection of players from his Oxford Orchestra, had become the new Festival conductor, advisor and occasional adjudicator in 1906 and, under him, the competitions flourished until 1914. Mrs Alexander Maitland (one of the Craig-Sellar sisters who founded the Festival) said of him "I first met Dr Allen after a Balliol concert at which I played in 1902 or 1903. I well remember how his astonishing vitality, his humour and his overpowering personality held us all spellbound. I felt that here was the person to vitalise our Festival".

Dr. Hugh Allen, caricatured at rehearsal

Well-known musicians such as Ralph Vaughan Williams, Adrian Boult and Hubert Parry supported the Festival in the pre-First World War era and special trains ferried audiences to and from Petersfield for the evening performances. Carriages also came to collect people from the Drill Hall at these early concerts – which must have provided a grand sight for local onlookers.

With the outbreak of war, plans for a Festival in 1915 were abandoned and the event was not resuscitated until 1920.

A further addition to the town's calendar of regular events came with the creation of a local branch of the Workers' Educational Association (WEA) in 1913. The national body had been established in 1903 "to promote the higher education of working men" and its lectures and courses still thrive today. In Petersfield, the first classes were in industrial history, and others were planned in political economy, the study of national life, English literature, sociology and citizenship. In their second year, the WEA took

John Haden Badley of Bedales

over the work which had been done since the 1890s by the Rural Polytechnic and introduced classes in shorthand and dressmaking and planned further courses in drawing and carpentry. Mr J.H. Badley (of Bedales) was elected their first President.

The Working Men's Club had continued to flourish in the Edwardian era, but suffered the setback of losing its premises in 1911 when the whole of Lord Hylton's estate was sold off, including the Institute where the club met. After an acrimonious debate on a possible solution, Colonel H.B. Hanna (the late president of East Hants Liberal and Labour Association and an author of books on military history) offered £500 to buy the premises [now the Scout Hut] and let it to the Club, but he was thwarted by a Mr Schwerdt of

The Working Men's Institute, built 1912

Alresford who obtained it and let it to The Liberal Club. Colonel Hanna and Mr C. J. P. Cave each offered £250 towards the building of a new Club and, after Mr Cave had also given a plot of land behind the Catholic Church for the purpose, a new Working Men's Institute took shape, much larger and grander than the first, and opened in 1912. It was designed by W. Bates White, the architect of the Electric cinema, and built in bungalow style, with a mixture of Swiss and Oriental design. It had space not only for all their previous activities, but boasted a top floor where there was to be a picture gallery and a museum; it also had a kitchen and a bathroom and, later, a bar. The building still exists today as the Petersfield Social Club, the oldest surviving club in the town.

Accidents

Car accidents still occurred quite frequently in Petersfield despite the small number of cars on the roads but, with slow-moving horse-drawn vehicles also on the town's roads, there were often problems for careless drivers. A bad collision took place in April 1911, for example, when one driver swerved to avoid a carriage and pair in College Street and

The Red Lion, catering for horses and motor cars

ended up hitting another car coming in the opposite direction. Although the two vehicles may not have been travelling at more than 8 m.p.h., the impact was such as to crack one of the engines, break a wheel and bend an axle and the smaller car ended up under the larger car.

Motorcycles ("motor bicycles") were also responsible for their share of accidents: in 1912, a horse trap carrying an Elstead couple and their daughter turned over when the horse took fright at a passing motorcycle and the family found themselves trapped underneath. They escaped serious injury but the wife did sustain a broken arm.

*A 1912 **Harley Davidson** motorcycle*

In July the same year, at Upper Bordean, all three victims of a car accident had to be taken to the Cottage hospital, where one of them, Walter Seward, subsequently died. The press talked of "an unprecedented haul of motorists in court". In Coronation week alone, there were 95 summonses issued to drivers and two courts had to sit simultaneously to clear any backlog; drivers, many of whom were coming from all parts of Hampshire to attend the Review of the Fleet in Portsmouth, were accused of speeding and driving without lights. Some were accused of "furious driving" and "wantonly driving", suggesting a general lack of road sense and a careless attitude towards other road users. Some more horrifying accidents involved cyclists and pedestrians who were struck or run over; a pony and trap in Charles Street was being driven at over 15 m.p.h. and thus posed a danger to the public; two motorcyclists collided on Ramshill near Broadlands, causing a fatality. One particularly nasty accident occurred when a horse and cab hit a passing car at the junction of Heath Road and the High Street and the horse's head smashed through the side window of the car.

Pony and trap in Dragon Street

1912 will forever be remembered as the year of the *Titanic* disaster. On the 24th April, nine days after the event, the *Hants and Sussex News* carried the following report:

> *After many days of weary waiting, the truth about the disaster to the Titanic, that supreme tragedy of the sea, has been told at last. It is a story that cannot be read*

without a feeling of horror. The narratives of the survivors bring the whole terrible scene to the eye of the mind, and it is impossible to think without a shudder of the awful happenings out there in the darkness, when the greatest and proudest ship that ever rode the ocean went crashing to her doom, and carried with her to the bottom of the Atlantic a precious freight of some 1,000 souls.

Only one person from Petersfield died in that tragedy, a Mr W.T. Stead. As elsewhere in the country, memorial services were conducted in the churches throughout the Petersfield district.

A serious accident much closer to home was the fire which caused extensive damage to Mr Thomas Privett's tailor's and outfitter's shop [now New Look] in the Square in 1913. This was a high-class store belonging to a well-known trader and UDC Councillor, who had suffered a similar disaster in 1907. Despite these two setbacks, the family (Thomas was succeeded by his son Edward) remained for over 70 years in the town. This is a 17th century house in origin, but whose front façade was rebuilt after the 1907 fire. Fortunately, although the 1913 fire had broken out in the night, the Fire Brigade had been able to attach a hosepipe to the hydrant in the Square nearby and put the fire out within an hour. The damage was estimated to be over £2,000.

Privett's Tailors and Outfitters, no. 2 High Street

Changes and improvements in public amenities in 1912

The installation of the new "augmented water scheme" in 1912 – with the supply of softer water from Oakshott – had at last alleviated the shortage felt for many years in the town and the proper cleansing of the Square after markets could proceed. This increase in the water supply was much appreciated by the Medical Officer of Health, Dr. H.M. Brownfield, who also commented in his annual report on the improved supply of milk and the good state of local slaughterhouses and bakehouses.

However, there were still problems with flooding in the High Street during heavy rains, especially in the area in front of the Dolphin Hotel [now Dolphin Court] as there was only one sump for rainwater to be cleared. At the other end of the town, the culverts in The Rushes [now the Winchester Road and Rushes Road area] were too small to disperse the water which frequently overflowed from the stream [now known as the Drum Stream]. This was a recurring problem and one which was to take many years to solve.

Lighting was improved in the same year, when the Petersfield and Selsey Gas Co. installed several new lamps in the High Street and the Square. These were single low-pressure gas lamps with 160 candle-power, with a triple-burner inverted refuge lamp at the bottom of the High Street, one light of which was to be kept burning all night. Similar lamps had replaced electric arc lamps in the approach to Waterloo Station and were being used largely in London and the suburbs. Four new lamps now stood at the corners of the Square.

At the Union Workhouse, there was a new Master and Matron team in charge: Mr and Mrs Ixer, who had previously worked in Suffolk, took over the running of the Institution and were to spend nearly thirty years there, before succumbing to the only bomb to fall on Petersfield in WW2 in 1940. They had a fluctuating number of inmates (between 50 and 60) to look after.

Long-standing members of the community and its institutions were not uncommon: in January 1912, Mr W.J. Tew retired from his position as Captain of the Petersfield Fire Brigade after 20 years of meritorious service, which also entitled him to a silver medal from the National Fire Brigade Union. He was also presented with a clock for his service by Captain W.P. Jacobs, his predecessor in the position of Captain. The following September, Mr Henry Way retired after twelve years' service at Petersfield Station, but, since his father had held the first position of Stationmaster at Liss Station when the Portsmouth Direct line was opened in 1859, the Way family could be said to have been acquainted with the London and South Western Railway Company for half a century. Henry Way had followed his father into the position at Liss before moving to Petersfield in 1900.

It is worth noting here, too, that it was in 1912 that the first National Insurance Act was passed by Parliament, one of the foundations of the Welfare State in Britain and part of the wider social reforms enacted by the Liberal government of 1906-1914. The Act provided for Health and Unemployment Benefits to be paid for the first time. The sick were entitled to receive treatment by a panel doctor and the unemployed could collect a weekly sum from a Labour Exchange. With these two elements of the Act, 2.3 million people were covered for unemployment benefit and almost 15 million for sickness benefit.

The National Insurance Act of 1912

Sir Heath Harrison

Heath Harrison was born in Lancashire 1857, but spent most of his life in Hampshire, at Le Court near Liss. Income from his shipping firm in Liverpool allowed him to become a very generous benefactor to numerous local causes. Local affairs were a major interest, and he was elected High Sheriff of Hampshire for the year 1916-7.

In 1911, Heath Harrison made a splendid memorial gift to Petersfield Cottage Hospital for a new "Edward VII Wing" primarily for paying patients, but also for others when not fully occupied. It had long been felt by the hospital's governing body that two wards should be made available to paying patients so that the poorer patients should not ever have their beds occupied, even in the case of accidents. In 1912, the hospital, under the direction of the Matron, Miss Farley, admitted 154 patients.

Heath Harrison House

Heath Harrison was created a Baronet in 1917. Between the wars, he served on the Board of Governors of Churcher's College, Petersfield. In 1932, the need for boarders prompted a gift from him and he presented his house and grounds (adjoining the playing fields) to the school. It first became Churcher's Prep School, then, later, the Headmaster's House. He died in 1934.

Deaths

Among the deaths occurring in the period before the First World War, there were those of three local dignitaries who had contributed widely to the community's life: Colonel H.B. Hanna, Dr A.W. Leachman and Mr J.P. Blair all died at an advanced age in 1914.

Col. Hanna died from a heart attack at his home, "Heathmere", in his 75th year. Brought up in one of the cottages at the top of Ramshill, he could remember the old days of stage coaches as they arrived at, and departed from, the town. His life revolved around the army – he spent 32 years of it in India at the time of the Mutiny in 1857, married there and returned home with his (English) wife in 1889. In Petersfield, he was known for his private philanthropy as well as his public efforts to further the welfare of the town and its inhabitants. He became a governor of the Cottage Hospital, actively supported the Working Men's Institute and the emergent WEA, the Literary and Debating Society, and was the first President of the Petersfield United Football Club. He was a staunch Liberal, made the cause of Woman's Suffrage his paramount political interest and also showed talent as a writer on military subjects.

"Fairley", from a painting c.1890

Dr A.W. Leachman passed away at his home, "Fairley", in College Street [since demolished] at the age of 76. For fifty years in Petersfield, he had fulfilled both his public duties as a General Practitioner and his private interests with diligence and affability. He was very much respected in the community. He was the medical officer for the Board of Guardians and for Petersfield itself, a governor of the Cottage Hospital, a UDC councillor, and a governor of Churcher's College. Dr. Leachman was a deeply religious man, served as Vicar's warden for 40 years, and took a leading part in all the developments of the parish and church of Petersfield. Politically, he was a Conservative and strongly supported the Primrose League and the cause of Woman's Suffrage. He was also active in the establishment of the Petersfield Musical Festival.

Mr J.P. Blair, like Col. Hanna, had sympathies for the poor and elderly; he died at the age of 80 at his home in Sussex Road. He had been one of the first photographers in the town, with a business in Lavant Street. He was not brought up in Petersfield, but had spent some time in business in America before coming here in the 1880s. His chief public work was for the Workhouse as a Guardian of the Poor and he frequently topped the polls at local Council elections. He was also instrumental in championing (at the UDC) the retention of the market in the Square. Like Col. Hanna, too, he was a strong Liberal, unallied to any church, and strictly pro-Temperance.

Unlike the kind-hearted and generous-natured Col. Hanna, he was at times irascible by temperament and over-enthusiastic in debate, to the detriment of his causes.

War!

General fears about Germany's growing militarism at this time were reflected in an article in the *Hants and Sussex News* in November 1912, reporting the publication of a book by Colonel H.B. Hanna, the local Liberal stalwart, entitled *Can Germany invade England?* His answer was an emphatic "no!", and he strove by means of an array of facts and figures to produce evidence that "we entertain no fears for her [Germany] to play on, that we know our strength and that, however far from all desire to use it from her detriment, we can and will maintain our naval supremacy, a supremacy on which our whole national life depends". Unfortunately, Col. Hanna's attempt to persuade his readers that relations with Germany should always be open and friendly failed to dissipate the embittered illusions which existed between the two countries.

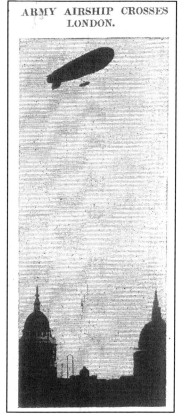

ARMY AIRSHIP CROSSES LONDON.

An army airship passes over London (photo in Hants and Sussex News, 1913)

A "Peace Meeting" held the same month in Petersfield was a further attempt to reduce the scaremongering which was agitating the population at large. However, the lecture on "The dangers of militarism" may have been intellectually satisfying, just as Col. Hanna's book had been, but these events did not prevent military training taking place, nor be seen to be taking place, and, a year later, a new army airship (the Delta), ostensibly on manoeuvres, was seen over Petersfield on its way to its base at Farnborough. When two naval balloons passed over Petersfield in the direction of Portsmouth, the trail rope of one of them became caught on a telegraph pole near Butser Hill – until a man climbed the pole and cut the balloon loose with a knife.

Aeroplanes were such a rarity in the skies that the one which flew over the town in 1912 excited everybody. It was flying from the direction of Portsmouth – perhaps heading for the airfield at Brooklands in Surrey, one of Britain's first airfields where the Sopwith Aviation Company had opened their school of flying that year.

During the summer of 1914, Petersfield pursued its normal timetable of events: the L&SWR announced an excursion train to London for the Harrod's sale; the

Excursion to Harrods Sale

Loyal Orange Institution produced a hundred marchers for their annual procession to King William's statue; the Horticultural Society held its annual show of flowers, fruit and vegetables; the WEA announced plans for classes in dairy work, butter- and cheese-making for September and October; and, even as late as August, Morton's shoeshop was advertising, in a totally inappropriate fashion, a "war" on prices. The war, although expected now, seemed a long way off; even the August Bank Holiday was extended to three days, to allow the government, faced with an imminent pan-European war, time to complete its financial arrangements.

In the first week of August, it was reported that Germany had declared war on Russia, its armies had crossed the French frontier at three points (without declaring war), and Luxemburg had been invaded. Days later, the *Hants and Sussex News* announced that England was now at war and the Royal Proclamation ordering the general mobilisation of all the forces of the Crown was posted at the Post Office in the High Street.

Mobilisation affected men, bicycles and horses: men left their employment to be recruited; the local 9th Hants (Cyclists) assembled in Petersfield Square and rode off to their headquarters at Horndean; horse owners were required to send their animals to one of two centres, Dark Hollow or the Police Station. There appeared to be no panic in Petersfield itself, but people did gather at the railway station each evening to buy the London papers for the latest news. Messages via the Exchange Telegraph were also received and posted in Mr Page's ironmonger's shop [now occupied by Bath Travel]. Farmers suffered from the loss of their men and horses and a mutual help arrangement was set up to bring in the harvest. Over 200 men were recruited in the first few days to the Petersfield Company of the 6th Hants regiment. Petersfield Scouts found themselves employed by the Post Office, the police and others in delivering messages in connection with the mobilisation of troops and the requisition of horses. Schoolchildren were

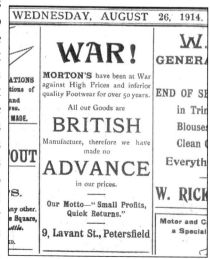

"War on prices" advert, 1914

employed on hop-picking duties. Businesses in town, such as Fuller's general stores in Lavant Street, the Reliance Steam Laundry in Frenchman's Road, and the town's coal merchants who relied on horse-drawn carts for deliveries, had to find alternative means of transport and delivery.

Like other towns, Petersfield opened a Roll of Honour to record the names of those who left on active service. Heading the list was Commander Loftus William Jones of HMS *Linnet* (later to be recorded as Petersfield's only VC holder). War reports and "Letters from the Front" now started to fill the whole of the back page of the *Hants and Sussex News* and a major recruiting drive was launched at the Corn Exchange in September by Lord Selborne, whose two younger sons were in India with the Hampshire Regiment.

Commander Loftus William Jones, V.C.

It has been estimated that about a thousand Petersfield men and women were recruited for all three services during the First World War; the town itself virtually became a garrison town, with troops quartered at the Drill Hall, the Corn Exchange, St. Peter's Hall, the Petersfield Laundry, Jacob's auction rooms, as well as in private houses. There was drilling on the Heath; daily marching through the streets; civilians learnt how to use a rifle; a canteen was set up in St. Peter's Hall; women began working in local business, industry and agriculture; and Mrs Bonham-Carter formed the Southern General Hospital of the Red Cross in Petersfield, supplementing the work of the Cottage Hospital and providing 400 beds for the wounded who returned from the war. Sadly, around 100 men from the town did not return.

Advert for the WWI *Women's Land Army*

Petersfield, inevitably, was never to be the same again.

Conclusion

Twenty-five years of history are bound to produce some radical changes in the lives of communities, and these have been examined in this volume. Clearly, the 1914-1918 war was also about to alter the structures of, and our attitudes towards, our society, but so had the previous quarter of a century. Certain developments within communities would be arrested, others accelerated by the war – social mobility, class consciousness, remarkable scientific and artistic accomplishments, for example – yet all these had been experienced and fostered in the Edwardian period too.

How, then, can these achievements be summarised and what can we legitimately ask ourselves about their impact on the succeeding years of the twentieth – or even twenty-first – century?

Both the tangible and sometimes almost imperceptible transformations in the social and political fabric of Petersfield and beyond have been dealt with, but what of the changing, underlying attitudes towards society itself? When the outside world impinges on the parochial, local issues are thrown into a lesser perspective. People's attitudes are naturally shaped by both global events and local preoccupations and, in Edwardian times, the wider perspective began to play an ever-increasing role in everyone's lives.

Might a changing attitude to our own "Britishness" be deduced from these findings? A comparison between the 1910s and the 2010s, for example, might elicit thoughts about Britain's place in the world: the Boer Wars were an overseas military venture which produced awkward and unpredictable consequences for us at home. Perhaps this was comparable to our own generation's experiences of war in the Middle East. Furthermore, with hindsight, the European war of 1914-18 might be seen to be the prelude to the even more globally reaching Second World War.

In economic terms, the relationship with the rest of Europe in the 1910s is comparable to our present preoccupations with China and India. Superpowers come and go. At home, sensitive issues such as immigration or scientific-versus-moral progress are still affecting us as they did a hundred years ago, and class differences are still a cause for anxieties among politicians.

In short, did we learn from the history of a hundred years ago?

-oOo-

Bibliography

An Edwardian Idyll?, Jonathan Wright, BBC History Magazine, Christmas 2010

A History of Christianity in Petersfield, (Petersfield Monographs no.4) PAHS, 2001

A school History of Hampshire, F. Clarke, Oxford, 1909

Churcher's College, Petersfield, J.H. Smith, Manchester Univ. Press, 1936

Edwardian Farm, Langlands, Goodman and Ginn, Pavilion Books, 2010

Edwardian Hampshire, (Notes from a lecture), Roger Ottewill, 2008

Family Journal – the war years, Betty Wardle, Southern Press, 1984

Harry Roberts – a Petersfield philanthropist, David Jeffery, 2009

High Street, Petersfield, (Petersfield Monographs no. 2), PAHS, 1984

Highways and Byways in Hampshire, D.H. Moutray Head, Macmillan, 1908

Looking back at Britain, Edwardian Summer, Reader's Digest, 2009

Looking Back at Britain, Victoria's final decade, Reader's Digest, 2009

Lost Voices of the Edwardians, Max Arthur, Harper, 2006

Petersfield and World War I, Doreen Binks, PAHS, 2007

Petersfield, a history and celebration, Kenneth Hick, Francis Frith, 2005

Petersfield Seen and Remembered, Des Farnham and Derek Dine, Hampshire County Library, 1982

Petersfield at War, David Jeffery, Sutton, 2004

Petersfield, a pictorial past, Sean Street, Ensign Publications, 1989

Petersfield – a Town History, G. Timmins, Lolaprint, 2009

Petersfield Music Makers,1901-1986, Marjorie Lunt and Mary Ray, PAHS 1986

Photographic View album of Petersfield and District, W. Emm & Son, Lavant St., 1935

Postwar Petersfield, David Jeffery, Sutton, 2006

Queen Victoria and her people, (Souvenir of the Diamond Jubilee), The Educational Supply Association, London, 1897

Some account of the history of Petersfield, E. Arden Minty, The Bodley Head, London, 1923

The Breweries of Petersfield, N.B. Redman, The Brewer, August 1994

The Buildings of England ; Hampshire: Winchester and the North, Michael Bullen et al., Yale University Press, 2010

The Condition of England, C.F.G. Masterman, Faber, 1909

The Edwardians, Roy Hattersley, Abacus, 2007

The History of Petersfield, Williams, Rev J., 1857, reproduced in *Petersfield, a pictorial Past* by Sean Street, Ensign Publications, 1989

The History of Churcher's College, Donald Brooks and Gillian Clarke, Baines Design (Herts), 2006

The Market Square, Petersfield, Mary Ray et al., PAHS, 2008

The Making of Modern Britain, Andrew Marr, Pan Books, 2009

The Portsmouth Road, Charles Harper, Chapman & Hall, 1895

The Sutton Companion to Local History, Stephen Friar, Sutton, 2004

The Victoria County History of the Counties of England (Volume 3: A History of the County of Hampshire) (1908) Reissued by the University of London, 1973

Village life in Hampshire in old picture postcards, Annette Booth, European Library, 1992

Documents consulted:

Censuses from 1891, 1901, 1911

Hants & Sussex News, 1890-1914

Kelly's Directory, 1895, 1911

PAHS (*Petersfield Area Historical Society*) *Bulletin*: selected articles from Spring 1976; Autumn 1977; Autumn 1978; Autumn 1979; Spring 1980; Autumn 1980; Autumn 1981; Autumn 1982; Spring 1983; Autumn 1983; Autumn 1984; Autumn 1985; Autumn 1991; Spring 1992; Autumn 1992; Autumn 1994; Autumn 1997; Spring 2008; Autumn 2008

Petersfield Urban District Council Minutes, 1897-1901, Hampshire Record Office

Petersfield, the official guide of the UDC, H. Logan & Co., 1909

"Way Back When", articles by "Natterjack", in *Petersfield Post*, 2006

Acknowledgments

This book could not have been produced without the help of many individuals and organisations. I have been lent pictures by the following:

David Allen; Doreen Binks; Pat Goodall; Chris Jacobs; Robert James; Jane Kirby; Edward Roberts; Prue Scurfield; Chris Shepheard; Petersfield Museum Archive; Photographic View Album of Petersfield and District, W. Emm & Son, Petersfield, 1935; L.E. Bradley; Goodes; A.W. Childs; Wessex Sound and Film Archive.

I must also gratefully acknowledge the help of various kinds which I have received from: Gordon Bray; Vaughan and Gill Clarke; Henry Edberg; Vicky Gibson (née Luker); Bill Gosney; Brenda Heath; Mike and Angela Kinsey; Tom Muckley; Tom Norgate; Roger Ottewill; Neil Pafford; Humphrey Sladden; Alastair Stewart; The Hampshire Record Office; Petersfield Library; Churcher's College.

Finally, my thanks go to my wife Irene and my daughter Anna-Louise for their proof-reading and indexing skills and their helpful advice during my two years of labour.

Index